Vygotsky at Work and Play

Vygotsky at Work and Play relates the discoveries and insights of Russian psychologist Lev Vygotsky to ordinary people and their communities. The author – working with her intellectual partner Fred Newman – has advanced a unique performance-based methodology of development and learning that draws upon a fresh and in some ways unconventional reading of Vygotsky. In this book, Holzman shows this methodology at work in key learning environments: psychotherapy, classrooms, out-of-school youth programs, and the workplace.

The book vividly describes Vygotskian-inspired programs involving thousands of people from a wide range of cultural backgrounds, ages and occupations. Interwoven in each chapter are discussions of Vygotsky's understandings of play, speaking, thinking, the zone of proximal development, the individual and the group. Holzman brings practice and theory together to provide a way forward for those who wish to liberate human development and learning from the confines of the social scientific paradigm, the institutional location of educational and psychological research, and the practices that derive from them.

Vygotsky at Work and Play presents a challenge to the underlying distinctions and boundaries of psychology, most significantly to the presumption of a cognitive–emotive divide, the notion of fixed identity, the privileging of the individual over the group and the instrumental nature of play and performance.

The book is essential reading for researchers and professionals in psychology, psychotherapy, cultural historical activity, social science, performance studies and education.

Lois Holzman is a developmental psychologist and Vygotskian scholar and practitioner and is Director at the East Side Institute for Group and Short Term Psychotherapy, New York.

Vygotsky at Work and Play

Lois Holzman

Routledge
Taylor & Francis Group

LONDON AND NEW YORK

First published 2009 by Routledge
27 Church Road, Hove, East Sussex BN3 2FA

Simultaneously published in the USA and Canada
by Routledge
270 Madison Avenue, New York, NY 10016

Routledge is an imprint of the Taylor & Francis Group, an Informa business

Copyright © 2009 Psychology Press

Typeset in Times by Garfield Morgan, Swansea, West Glamorgan
Printed and bound in Great Britain by TJ International Ltd, Padstow,
Cornwall
Cover design by Lisa Dynan

British Library Cataloguing in Publication Data
A catalogue record for this book is available from the British Library

Library of Congress Cataloging-in-Publication Data
Holzman, Lois, 1946–
   Vygotsky at work and play / Lois Holzman.
      p. cm.
   Includes bibliographical references and index.
   ISBN 978-0-415-42294-9 (hb)
   1. Vygotskii, L. S. (Lev Semenovich), 1896–1934. I. Title.
   BF109.V95H65 2009
   150.92–dc22

                                                            2008027287

ISBN 978-0-415-42294-9 (Hbk)

For Jovan Savić
who worked and played for a
revolutionary psychology
1937–2006

We must not make things stand still in order that they might be studied.

(The character Lev Vygotsky in the play, *Life Upon the Wicked Stage*, by Fred Newman)

Contents

Acknowledgements

My appreciation/thanks/gratitude to the following people:

For encouragement, support and all manner of assistance – Gail Elberg, Dan Friedman, Kate Hanselmans, Carrie Lobman, Susan Massad, Melissa Meyer, and Fred Newman.

For the incredible work they do creating development – Fred Newman and the therapists of the Social Therapy Group; Dan Friedman, Gabrielle Kurlander, Pam Lewis, Brian Mullin and all of the All Stars Project staff, donors and volunteers; Cathy Salit and the Performance of a Lifetime staff and trainers; the East Side Institute all-volunteer faculty and staff; Lenora Fulani.

For careful reading and helpful suggestions on the initial proposal – the reviewers.

For a terrific editorial and production process – Lucy Kennedy, Sharla Plant and the entire Routledge team.

Acknowledgments

Foreword

"Why didn't I pack my computer," I ask in dismay. The accumulated e-mail messages now approximate a mountain that I simply cannot face. And, there is also an unfinished manuscript that I have promised to a journal, and several phone messages that demand "immediate" attention. Most significantly, there is tomorrow's class for which I must prepare. My plight is not uncommon. For most of my scholarly friends, this is normal life. We always seem to be running an up-hill race in which we are perpetually behind. We seldom take the time to look backward, to ask ourselves about the trajectory, how the pieces fit with one another, and the accumulated lessons we have derived from our efforts. And this is regrettable.

It is against this backdrop that I was graced with the arrival of Lois Holzman's manuscript, *Vygotsky at Work and Play*. Here was an enormously active scholar and practitioner who did take the time to reflect on her activities of the past years. The results should be an invitation to all of us. In this work, Holzman reflects on her many endeavors over recent decades – her work in therapeutic settings, in schools, in after-school programs, in performance programs for adolescents, in organizations, and more. She locates the ways in which these endeavors build upon each other, the implicit and pervasive values they exhibit, and the growth in her own theoretical views over the years. In many respects her concern in this book is with human development, and in its exposition it brilliantly demonstrates just such development in action.

One of the most engaging aspects of this book is the way in which Holzman ties these various endeavors together theoretically, and her illumination of the way her theoretical understanding has developed through her practice. This is a most important aspect of the book, as the place of theory in the social sciences has been significantly eroded over the years. It is erosion to which the positivist/empiricist expansion first contributed. Increasingly, for scholars, the strong emphasis was placed on contributions to the empirical literature. Professional success depended on published research outcomes. Theoretical and metatheoretical discussion became moribund. The post-modern turn was additionally critical of theory, but in this case of traditional claims to theory as truth bearing. Theory was again thrown into question. However, in the present work, Holzman shows us how theory has played a significant role in orienting her activities. She demonstrates the way in which theory entered into the discussions that accompanied the unfolding of the various initiatives. And, most significantly, she lets us see how the activities helped her to expand and enrich the theoretical views with which she began. And now, we as readers are invited to crawl into this theoretical space, and to explore its implications for our own pursuits.

For my own part I find these developments in theory, and their application to practice, enormously exciting. The work is informed at base by the writings of Lev Vygotsky. These writings have long functioned as a radical critique of mainstream cognitive psychology, embracing as it does a view of human cognition as self-contained, and biologically determined. For Vygotsky, human thought is fundamentally dependent on the socio-cultural context. Social action is not, then, driven by cognitive mechanisms beyond human control. Rather, for Vygotsky and a dynamic group of like minded scholars, social transformation may be achieved through critical analysis and collaborative activity. While Holzman's demonstration of Vygotsky at work and play is illuminating, what I find especially exciting is the direction in which she takes Vygotsky's work. Many psychologists have tended to fold Vygotskian theory into an individualist frame. That is, they have resonated with passages in Vygotsky that focus on "higher mental functions." On this account, the social world must be taken into account, but primarily as a determining influence on mental life. In itself, the social world is of no special interest. Holzman reverses the emphasis, and with important results. If individual action emerges from a social source, then it is through social processes that transformation may be achieved. And this transformation is the essence of human development.

Thus, for example, Holzman is not content to view the *zone of proximal development* in its more individualist and cognitive terms, that is, as the difference between what the individual may accomplish in terms of existing cognitive functioning and what may be accomplished through the help of another. Rather, Holzman introduces us to the concept of a *zone* of *emotional development*, in which she emphasizes the development of emotion in collaborating with others in building functional relationships. The strong emphasis, then, is on the collaborative process, with individual development carried in its wake.

As Holzman also demonstrates, the shift in emphasis from cognition to emotion has significant implications for practice. By including the emotions, Holzman is able to make Vygotsky relevant in new and important ways to practices in therapy, education, and daily life. Further, from Holzman's standpoint, this shift to the social implications of Vygotsky's work puts an entirely new light on the function of play in social life. It is in play that challenges are made to "things as they are," and it is through playing together that development is hastened. At this point, the entire spectrum of the arts becomes relevant to human development, and to practices in schools and organizations. Improvisation in daily relations becomes a key to continuing development.

In the end, Holzman calls into question the entire, individualist centered tradition. She rightfully sees that the individual cut away from relationships is an empty vessel. And it is in this move that I find Holzman's journey an especially significant stimulus for my own work. I am just completing an effort that has been incubating for over a decade. This work, *Relational Being, Beyond the Individual and Community*, will now bear the traces of relationship with Holzman's inspiring book. I am indeed grateful.

Ken Gergen
Swarthmore College, USA

Preface

I met Lev Vygotsky when I was an emerging academic, a becoming developmental psychologist/psycholinguist. I became radically political and introduced Vygotsky to my political mentor, who was also a philosopher. I left academia to work with him outside of the mainstream, bringing Vygotsky with me.

My first mentor was Lois Bloom, a researcher and teacher who I worked with in the mid 1970s when I was a graduate student in the developmental psychology program at Columbia University. Lois taught me that to learn how children learn to speak and develop language we had to leave the laboratory and go into their homes and play groups. We had to spend time with toddlers, playing with them, talking with them, performing with them. I learned that context matters, that children don't do the same things in a laboratory that they do at home, that their talk is coordinated with what they are doing and who and what they are doing it with. I learned from working with Lois that qualitative research can be as rigorous – indeed, more rigorous – than quantitative research. Lois helped me to love research. She projected me out of the lab, and that has been the foundation of everything I have done since.

My second mentor, with whom I did postdoctoral work at Rockefeller University in the late 1970s, was Michael Cole. Mike taught me that laboratory experiments on human cognition cannot be ecologically valid because you can't see the social-cultural nature of cognition in the lab. He also was the first person to make me aware that science in general, and the social sciences and psychology in particular, are political and that the research we psychologists do can be practically relevant. And Mike introduced me to that very practical and very political social scientist, Lev Vygotsky. Both of those introductions – to Vygotsky and to the political nature of psychology – set the stage for my third mentor, Fred Newman.

I met Fred when I was completing my dissertation and beginning to work with Cole. Fred was a philosopher who had left academia during the late 1960s to do political and community organizing. He also had created a radical type of therapy, social therapy, informed by his background in philosophy of science and Marxism. Fred taught me many things through the decades of our continuous collaboration. One thing he did was give me a way into the world. Lois Bloom and Mike Cole both encouraged me to leave the laboratory. But while we may have been sitting in a playroom or family living room instead of a university lab, we brought the experimental mindset and method of the laboratory with us. What Fred showed me was a way to take the lab out of life. He invited me to develop a way to study the world through actively engaging in changing it. With Fred, I came to realize that my passion for human development came not just from intellectual curiosity but also from my belief that human beings must find a way to develop if our species is to survive and thrive, and from my desire to contribute to this revolutionary activity.

Having Fred as my mentor – we have been working together for over 30 years now – has not only transformed what I do, it transformed who I am. I feel I am a better scientist for being a builder and co-creator of what I study, a better researcher for getting the laboratory out of life. Doing this does not negate any of the lessons and gifts provided by my first two mentors. The socio-cultural situatedness of learning and development, the need for psychology to be ecologically valid, the political nature of psychology, the contemporary significance of Lev Vygotsky – these teachings of Bloom and Cole have all been deepened and developed by being taken out of academia and brought into the lives of ordinary people. They have become part of the activity that Fred and I, and many hundreds of others, engage in. It is I who brought Vygotsky to Fred Newman and inspired him to turn his revolutionary and philosophical eye toward his works. It is Fred who has encouraged me and others to develop the living Vygotoskyism evidenced throughout this book.

I once wrote that my dream was to make Lev Vygotsky a household word. I was talking about my work with the experimental Barbara Taylor School (discussed in Chapter 3), and wanting to bring Vygotsky to the children and families of Harlem so that together we could use him to reinitiate their development and radicalize their schooling. The essay which I wrote appeared as a chapter in an academic book on social constructionism and organizational behavior, hardly a venue that would further my cause! And while the book I am now writing and you are now reading may have a slightly wider audience, its contribution to my dream will also be minimal. No matter. In the 8 years since I wrote that chapter, Vygotsky has spread not only through Harlem, but dozens of communities across the USA and other countries.

In the earliest stages of this book, an anonymous reviewer took issue with part of my rationale for writing the book. I wrote that Vygotsky is a living force in the lives of tens of thousands of ordinary people – a statement that to the reviewer read more like a blurb than part of a scientific text. In the course of writing I kept going back to this criticism, as it raises issues central to the theme of the book. Are fact and value to be distinguished? If so, on what criteria? And what of objectivity and subjectivity? What constitutes a scientific statement and evidence for it? Is science free of persuasion? Of subjectivity? If I had written that Freud or Piaget was a living force in people's lives, would the distinction have been noted? Presumably, no psychologist would question the facticity of such a claim. But that still leaves open not only how one would go about gathering evidence for it but also what purpose there would be for doing so – other than persuasion!

Vygotsky at Work and Play is a qualitative inquiry, a life history of intertwined relationships, projects and communities in which Vygotsky plays a key role. Mostly, it is my story of bringing Vygotsky from the scientific laboratory to ordinary people and their communities, and of what I and others have created with him. It is the story of a unique kind of intervention research and the conflicted ways in which institutionalized psychology and educational research relate to it. Like all that we have created with Vygotsky, this book is consciously and thoroughly subjective. It is written to inform, provoke and persuade readers to the value of the "Vygotskian–Newman–Holzman tool-and-result practice of method" – a process of creating environments for development. The book tries to show what it looks like when ordinary children, youth and adults engage in this process in a variety of everyday life settings. The new activity they create is their (and the world's) development. It is, as well, a practical-critical questioning of the distinctions, dichotomies and boundaries of the existing ways of doing psychology and the assumptions underlying them. As such, *Vygotsky at Work and Play* is essentially a performatory text, simultaneously a part of and a reflection on the conceptual revolution underway in psychology and the broader culture.

Some of the concepts discussed in other books on Vygotsky are rarely mentioned here or discussed with a quite different "take." For example, I spend little time on the topic of mediation and mediational tools, a major contribution Vygotsky is said to have made to understanding human development. Another example is the zone of proximal development (zpd), which I treat as an activity of social creativity rather than as a characteristic of an individual. Other concepts are possibly unique to my work, taken from Vygotsky and radically transformed. Examples of this are completion, stemming from Vygotsky's claim that thought is completed in the word, and performance, originating in his characterization of play as allowing the child to perform as if a head taller. And, most important is the introduction of tool-and-result methodology, taken from Vygotsky's description of what he referred to as his search for method.

Dozens of scholars have written about Vygotsky's life, theory and method. I have learned a great deal from the interpretations of Vygotsky by many of them, especially Jerome Bruner, Michael Cole, Joe Glick, Vera John-Steiner, Alex Kozulin, Carl Ratner, Dorothy Robbins, Anna Stetsenko, Jaan Valsiner, Rene van der Veer and James Wertsch.[1] The academic literature is filled with historical and theoretical debates, critiques and controversy among these writers and others. While I have sometimes joined these debates and have written my share of critique, you will find little of it in the following pages. I want my story and interpretation of Vygotsky to inspire, provoke and/or resonate with you on its own, without being buttressed by any critical comments I might have on the work of others. To do otherwise, I feel, would be antithetical to the philosophy and method of my inquiry and to the practices that are its subject. I urge interested readers to approach the ideas of others on their own merit, unencumbered by my interpretation of them.

Chapter 1

Methods(s) and Marx(s)

> An old style can be translated, as it were, into a newer language; it can, one might say, be performed afresh at a tempo appropriate to our own times.
>
> (Ludwig Wittgenstein, *Culture and Value*, 1984, p. 60e)

THE COGNITIVE PARADIGM AND THE COGNITIVE–EMOTIVE DIVIDE

While I may have encountered the word *paradigm* before then, it wasn't until I had already earned my PhD (in 1977) that I remember paying any attention to it. For whatever reasons, the book that popularized the term, Kuhn's (1962) monograph *The Structure of Scientific Revolutions*, wasn't on any of my graduate school course reading lists. I think things have changed enough in 30 years so that this is not your first encounter with the concept.

Although it has specific meanings in some academic disciplines, Kuhn's characterization of paradigm as "an entire constellation of beliefs, values, techniques, and so on shared by the members of a given community" (1962, p. 175) is generally accepted and popularly used, along with *model, system of thought* and *worldview*. In his description of how science develops, and through examples from the history of physics, biology, medicine and other areas of science, Kuhn outlined an historical process that included extended "moments" of the revolutionizing of scientific thought, what he called *paradigm shifts*. These are not merely revisions of individual theories; rather, they change everything – the way scientists view their subject matter, the terminology of the field, the questions that are considered valid, and the methods by which particular theories are to be evaluated. Commonly cited paradigm shifts are those from a Ptolemic (earth-centered) to a Copernican (sun-centered) cosmology, and from a Newtonian to an Einsteinian physics. Within philosophical, scientific and social scientific circles there has been a sustained debate on the validity and applicability of Kuhn's characterization and terminology outside of the physical sciences. Meanwhile, Kuhn's terminology has entered the vocabulary of nearly every academic discipline and professional field. Whether overused or not, I find the concepts of paradigm and paradigm shifts useful in understanding Vygotsky, and you will encounter them frequently throughout this chapter and beyond. For what I have found in Vygotsky's attempt to create a new human science paradigm are the seeds of a *nonparadigmatic* approach to human life. The path to discovery was an unlikely one.

Thirty years ago I brought Vygotsky to Fred Newman, the creator of an unusual therapeutic approach known as social therapy. Social therapy was a few years old then, and completely new to me. I was thrilled to have discovered Vygotsky in my own search to understand the complexity of the relationships between language, thought, learning and development. I was intrigued by social therapy and Newman's overall approach to people, institutions, ideas, life and revolutionary change. Meeting Vygotsky had changed my world. Meeting Newman had changed my world. Understandably, I very much wanted the two to meet each other! I was convinced that bringing Vygotsky and Newman together would yield something unique. They didn't disappoint me.

Once I succeeded in interesting him in Vygotsky, Newman, who was a philosopher by training, enlisted me – a developmental psychologist – in an exploration of Vygotsky's approach and ideas in relation to social therapy. The "results" have been deep and broad. As a psychotherapy, social therapeutic practice has become more radical and more relevant for being Vygotskianized. Additionally, social therapeutics more broadly has emerged as an effective human development methodology applicable to a wide variety of educational and cultural settings, institutions and communities in the USA and other countries. These developments have yielded new understandings of the paradigmatic constraints of contemporary, philosophically overdetermined psychology and how to break free of them.[1]

Many, many others have critiqued what psychology has become and presented their arguments for alternative paradigms.[2]

Vygotsky's popularity from the last quarter of the twentieth century up to the present can certainly be understood in this way. His writings have served to inspire and support a paradigm shift in our understanding of human development and learning from ahistorical, acultural, individualistic unfoldings to cultural-historical socially created processes (often referred to as CHAT – cultural-historical activity theory – or socio-cultural activity theory). There is an active global community of scholars informed by Vygotsky whose research methods and findings are working to effect a qualitative change in how psychologists see. To me, this is one of the most important and exciting things happening in the social sciences and educational research. And while I am counted among this community of scholars (which is something very important to me), there is a way in which my work differs qualitatively.

Rather than work to effect a paradigm shift in psychology, my efforts are to effect a shift away from paradigmism altogether.[3] Activity theory, as it has come to be practiced and articulated in the work my colleagues and I do, is more and other than a new paradigm. It is a new ontology that can do away with the need for paradigms. This radical position against paradigmism (and epistemology, explanation and knowing) is a lot of what Newman and I write about, as we urge others to turn their attention to creating new "ways of seeing" *synthesized* with discovering new "ways of being" (Holzman, 1999; Newman, 2000a; Newman and Holzman, 1996/2006, 1997). Vygotsky was not a fellow antiparadigmist, yet his attempts to do away with some of the most deeply rooted dualistic ways of seeing human development have greatly informed and advanced our work.

Vygotsky traversed several dualistic divides: biology and culture, behavior and consciousness, thinking and speaking, learning and development, and individual and social.[4] He refused to accept the foundational dualism of this kind of psychological conceptualization and argued forcefully against it, urging instead a method of dialectics. His writings on these matters have been noted and debated, some extensively, by Vygotskian researchers and historians. Far less recognized but equally important is Vygotsky's challenge to psychology's dualistic conceptualization of cognition and emotion. This aspect of Vygotsky's thinking has been critical in my work, and I often have wondered why my academic colleagues do not follow suit.

Which brings us back to psychotherapy. Vygotsky's ideas have been studied in relation to dozens of intellectual disciplines and areas of professional practice, but psychotherapy, emotions and emotional development are not among them. With few exceptions, contemporary Vygotskians stay clear of that area. As for psychotherapy researchers and practitioners, unless they have come across writings on social therapeutics, the theoretical writings of psychologist John Shotter (1993a, 1993b, 2000, 2006) or the recent writings of narrative therapist Michael White (2007), it is doubtful they have even heard of Vygotsky.[5] What are we to make of this phenomenon – that the work of such a seminal thinker, dubbed "the Mozart of psychology" (Toulmin, 1978), frequently uttered in the same breath as Piaget and Freud, and ranked within the hundred most referenced psychologists (Haggbloom et al., 2002) has not been vigorously applied to the largest area (in impact and in sheer number of psychologists) within the discipline of psychology? I think it speaks loudly of the same paradigmatic constraints and biases that make it so difficult to see the significance of how Vygotsky understands cognition and emotion. For, in order to appreciate Vygotsky's challenge to psychology's dualistic conceptualization of cognition and emotion, psychotherapy – where emotion occupies center stage – is where one would have to go.

Emotion has a long history in Western culture of being considered second rate – inferior to cognition, the enemy of rationality and an attribute not of men, but of women. In spite of the significant contributions feminist psychologists and philosophers have made in exposing the male biases of accepted conceptions of being human, the overall cultural environment of psychology has remained paradigmatically male and cognitively overdetermined.[6] I believe this is no less the case among socio-cultural psychologists, including those who have been greatly influenced by Vygotsky. As for psychotherapy, the area of psychology most identified with emotion, it is generally thought of as soft science, or not science at all. This assessment is applauded by those who agree and relate to psychotherapy as an art or cultural activity, and lamented by those who disagree and work to advance its scientific credentials. Especially in the last two decades, the profession as a whole has bowed to pressure or taken up the mantle (depending on one's point of view) to become more "scientific" (objective, measurable, "evidence-based," etc.), even as female psychotherapists now outnumber their male counterparts, a trend also noted for psychology as a whole (*American*

Psychological Association, 2005). While the shift to relationality (often making use of the feminist conception of connection, as put forth in *Toward a New Psychology of Women*, Miller, 1976) that is occurring in the profession is a welcome innovation, in the overall conservative environment in which it is taking place it is not only marginalized but vulnerable to being cast in cognitive terms.

My focus on the cognitive–emotive split is not meant to imply that it is, in some abstractly hierarchical sense, more significant than the other dualistic divides Vygotsky traversed. Rather, it is woven throughout this text because of its unique importance to the Vygotsky that my colleagues and I have discovered and been inspired by.

WHY METHOD?

I write this book as a "creative imitation" of Vygotsky, the revolutionary, the Marxist, the psychologist, the educator. Because I am a psychologist and do not like what psychology as an institution, industry and discipline promulgates. I think that nearly all of its theory and practice – generated in a misguided effort to emulate the natural and physical sciences – goes against the stated mission of its largest professional organization, the American Psychological Association (APA), which is to promote "health, education, and the public welfare" (http://www.apa.org/about/). Because I am an educator and lament the ineptitude and impenetrability of the current educational system and the harm it is doing to children, educators, families and the world. Because as a psychologist and educator I have learned that most people, including fellow psychologists and educators, have similar opinions about how psychology and education are misguided and misguiding, but do not know what to do other than go along with how things are and make the best of it. And because I have learned first hand that not knowing what to do is often the best place to be to create innovation and effect change. Vygotsky has helped me and, I suspect, many others to not know. How he has been helpful is not straightforward, for he was, in many ways, as invested in knowing as anyone of his time and place. But he did step outside what was known even though he did not know how before he did it.

Lev Vygotsky was, in a word (or two), a revolutionary scientist of the last century (Bruner, 1996; Newman and Holzman, 1993;

Wertsch, 1985). He worked brilliantly and painstakingly to understand what needed to be understood to make profound and progressive social change. For him, much of what needed to be understood was how human beings learn and develop and create culture. That he managed at all to "think outside the box" of the dominant worldview of his time is remarkable. For, the modernist scientific view and its conceptions of truth, systemization, generalization, explanation, measurement and teleology not only shaped the developing social sciences, but also overdetermined the Marxism and communism of the 1920s and 1930s. As a Marxist, Vygotsky could not help but to buy into the belief that human liberation would have a scientific face. Read today, Vygotsky's writings show both acceptance and struggle against this intellectual constraint, which is both sobering and inspiring to me.

Early on in conceptualizing this book I thought I would begin by drawing parallels between the "crisis in psychology" that Vygotsky was addressing in the early twentieth century and the one that we who live in the early twenty-first century are faced with. So I went back and re-read a thoughtful essay on this same topic by Rieber and Wollock, which appears as the "Prologue" to Volume 3 of Vygotsky's collected works (1997). I wondered if I had anything to add, given the passage of a decade since they wrote.

Rieber and Wollock characterize the two crises as formally similar but substantially different.

> When Vygotsky was writing the "Crisis," psychology was only at the start of its popularization in Europe and America. Then as now the profession was chaotic, but for a different reason. At that time it was because the profession was everywhere undeveloped, though full of brilliant possibilities. Today it is because the field is overpopulated and its general level is mediocre.
>
> (Rieber and Wollock, 1997, p. x)

That seems hard to disagree with, but it is seriously under-historicized. In Vygotsky's time, psychology was not merely young – its course toward natural, social or human science was uncertain, and that uncertainty was an important reason for the urgency with which Vygotsky addressed the issue. Furthermore, what was to become psychology's massive influence as an industry and its incredible success as a means of social control was unimaginable.

Given that the entire world, and not just the role psychology plays in the world, has completely transformed politically, economically, scientifically, technologically and culturally since the 1920s, I do not think there is much to be learned from comparing the two crises. It might, in fact, not even make sense to speak of a current crisis in psychology at all. We live in a world in which psychology rules. It is the authority that is appealed to in the classroom, the courtroom, the clinic, the personnel office, the organization, the advertising and media industry, the armed forces and the family. I no longer think there is a crisis in psychology. In fact, psychology is doing just fine, while the world mess is getting worse. And that's the crisis.

In that period of uncertainty as to the direction psychology would take, Vygotsky was raising fundamental questions about science. His conviction that there needed to be a general (unifying) and systematic psychology (Vygotsky, 1997, pp. 233–343) came directly from his era's conception of science as a body of knowledge/inquiry bounded by a core set of agreed upon conceptions and explanatory principles. His intellectual contribution mirrored and contributed to late nineteenth and early twentieth century philosophy of science. Viewed in light of contemporary dialogues in the history and philosophy of science and the newer interdisciplinary field of science studies, his thinking on the matter often appears simplistic. Rather than this being a criticism of him, it is a reminder that he was a product of his time. This is, in my experience, often forgotten or overlooked in discussions of Vygotsky and contemporary work inspired by him.

One way the forgetting or overlooking of Vygotsky's social-historical location looks is when he is judged by contemporary standards of scholarship or in light of twenty-first century scientific developments and cultural, political or historical understandings. (Is Vygotsky's empirical work replicable? Was he truly a psychologist? Was Vygotsky racist? Was he a Marxist? Was his work ideologically driven?) Another manifestation of this "forgetting" is assessing who or what of the current day is worthy of being called Vygotskian – and assuming that the closer to Vygotsky's own work, the better. It seems to me that one could just as plausibly argue the opposite; namely, that the closer contemporary work is to Vygotsky's original work, the less "Vygotskian" it should be considered, given that his was first and foremost a cultural-historical endeavor and that historical conditions have transformed so thoroughly. This seems in keeping with Vygotsky's life activity, from what we have been told of it, including his perspective that "a revolution solves only those tasks raised by history" (Vygotsky, quoted in frontpiece, Levitan, 1982). For Vygotsky those tasks were raised by the first successful communist revolution, and he devoted himself to revolutionizing the psychology of his day to solve those tasks. His failed effort (inseparable from communism's failure) contains remarkable methodological breakthroughs that are useable in efforts to revolutionize today's psychology to solve the tasks history is raising for us.

The question Vygotsky posed about human development and learning and how to study it was a task raised by history. First, the transformation from a feudal Russia to a Soviet Union characterized by a planned economy was a monumental task. Creating a new culture involved facing very serious "learning and development" challenges – among them, nearly universal illiteracy, cultural differences among the hundreds of ethnic groups that formed the new nation, absence of services for those unable to participate fully in the formation of the new society, and millions of abandoned and homeless children who roamed the country. Vygotsky and his colleagues were a part of a great real-life experiment in creating the hoped-for new society (see, for example, Bruner, 2004; Friedman, 1990; Newman and Holzman, 1993; Stetsenko, 2004; Wertsch, quoted in Holzman, 1990, pp. 21–22).

Second, in posing this question, Vygotsky was treating science as a cultural phenomenon open to scrutiny and radical transformation. Science as social-cultural-historical activity was what concerned him. By the 1920s, the field of psychology was well on its way to becoming an empirical and experimental science, and questions of method and units of analysis were hotly debated. For example, would following the experimental path mean excluding from psychological investigation the very nature of human consciousness? Vygotsky was not willing to give up the study of consciousness (nor the "higher psychological processes" that are its manifestations). Nor was he willing to settle for two kinds of psychology (a subjective one for mental events and an objective one for nonmental events) or one psychology if it bypassed consciousness by reducing mental events to nonmental ones. Both options, he argued extensively, rested on an erroneous belief in an objectivist epistemology, which, in effect, denies science as a human (meaning-making) activity and mistakenly treats human beings as natural phenomena. For Vygotsky, psychology as a human science could not develop so long as it was based in objective–subjective dualism.

This brought Vygotsky to question the very method of scientific inquiry. (By method what is meant here is the entire methodological approach, not a specific research technique.) The method of natural science might work for studying natural phenomena, but it cannot be a good fit for the study of human beings. A psychology with a natural science method contains "an insoluble methodological contradiction. It is a natural science about unnatural things" and produces "a system of knowledge which is contrary to them" (Vygotsky, 1997a, p. 300). A scientific study of human beings required a nondualistic method, a precondition of which was a nondualistic *conception of method*. Here is how Vygotsky phrased the challenge:

> The search for method becomes one of the most important problems of the entire enterprise of understanding the uniquely human forms of psychological activity. In this case, the method is simultaneously prerequisite and product, the tool and the result of the study.
>
> (Vygotsky, 1978, p. 65)

Vygotsky is proposing a radical break with the accepted scientific paradigm in which method is a tool that is applied and yields results. In this case, the relation between tool and result is linear, instrumental and dualistic, what Newman and I call *tool for result methodology* (Newman and Holzman, 1993). Vygotsky proposes a qualitatively different conception of method – not a tool to be applied, but an activity (a "search") that generates both tool and result at the same time and as continuous process. Tool and result are not dualistically separated, neither are they the same or one thing. Rather, they are elements of a dialectical unity/totality/whole. Method to be practiced, not applied, is what Vygotsky was advocating. To capture the dialectical relationship of this new conception, Newman and I call this *tool-and-result methodology* (Newman and Holzman, 1993). This new conception of method, it should be obvious, is neither objective nor subjective, but something outside that dualistic box. That is its strength and potential power. As I will discuss in more detail in later chapters, Newman and I believe that this tool-and-result methodology is not only the relevant one for studying human development but as well is an apt and rich characterization of the activity of human development itself. No doubt the seeds of this idea were already there in the work we were doing; our reading of Vygotsky gave articulation to them. We could say that, in Vygotskian fashion, his words "completed" our thinking (Vygotsky, 1987, pp. 250–251).[7]

THE PROBLEM WITH PROBLEMS

The Western scientific worldview is filled with problems. I mean that literally – problems are the "stuff" of life. People are socialized to see and understand themselves and others in terms of, and in the language of, problems. And with problems come – even if not always realized – solutions. In ordinary language, problems imply possible solutions just as questions imply possible answers. Identifying problems and coming up with solutions to them is the hallmark of good science, good education, good government, good diplomacy and good living. Problems are what we are taught to see; solutions are what we are taught to search for. This way of seeing and mode of thinking might be needed to fix cars and build houses, but there is little evidence that they are effective when it comes to human development issues, such as raising children, living peacefully or eliminating poverty. And yet, the problem-solution paradigm prevails, overdetermining and severely limiting the human capacity to continuously create the world. The paradigm has become the problem.

Vygotsky's tool-and-result method provides a way out of the problem (but not a solution). For the methodology with which to tackle a world filled with problems is an instrumental one. Tool for result methodology is the epistemological counterpart to the ontology of problems and solution; it is essentially a problem-solving approach. In contrast, tool-and-result methodology rejects this way of viewing and living in the world, in favor of a more unified, emergent and continuous process approach.

Nowhere are problems and paradigms more misplaced than in the practice of psychotherapy, an institution dominated by the problematizing of emotional life/activity. For the patient/client, going to a therapist means that something is wrong, and she or he will be judged according to her or his "presenting problem." For the mainstream psychotherapist, the task is to find the solution to the problem, first by naming it and then by going through with the patient/client a process of discovering the cause or source of the problem, by prescribing medication or by some combination of the two. Institutionalized psychotherapy is so organized around problems that if you do not have one that is identifiable according to the fourth edition of the *Diagnostic and Statistical Manual of Mental Disorders* (APA, 2000), you can be denied treatment. (One example that has received popular media coverage is Ednos, which stands for "eating disorder not otherwise specified," as reported on in the *New York Times* article entitled, "Sorry. Your Eating Disorder Doesn't Meet Our Criteria" on 30 November 2004 by Henig.)

While there has been much criticism of the insistence on diagnosis as a requirement for psychotherapy, including pleas to abandon the medical model and view psychotherapy as an art and not a science,[8] there is less critical discussion on the problem-solution paradigm that underlies it. (Pointing out that the person is not the problem, but "has" a problem for example, does not deny the problem-solution paradigm.) I suspect that the cognitive bias is at play here, as the problem-solution paradigm is, essentially, a cognitive model of emotionality. As I will show in Chapter 2, Vygotsky's attempt to circumvent cognition–emotion dualism inspired the further development of the tool-and-result methodology of social therapy.

BEHAVIOR

As it developed over this century, the discipline of psychology took a very different path from the one Vygotsky advocated. It virtually ignored the methodological issues he raised and, instead, created itself in the image of the natural and physical sciences. It rejected dialectics in favor of linearity and causality. It adopted the dualistic conception of method as something to be applied (tool for result methodology) and rejected Vygotsky's search (tool-and-result methodology). It promoted an understanding of human beings that combines a natural science view (we are a behaving species) with a technological metaphor (we are like machines). Having fashioned the image of human beings as individuals separated from each other and our environment, psychologists created for themselves the task of figuring out how any of us ever get "socialized."

Having conceptualized an "inner world" and "outer reality," they had to posit theories, devise research strategies and conduct investigations to answer the puzzling questions of how the "inner" gets externalized and the "outer" becomes internalized.

Kurt Danziger has written extensively about how American psychology created itself in the image of the natural sciences in a little over 100 years. His book, *Naming the Mind: How Psychology Found its Language*, is especially useful in showing how psychology created its units of analysis and conceptions through its mystifying and ahistorical discourse. Exposing this, one can see that psychology had nothing "natural" to talk about, but only what it has invented:

> Psychological research is supposed to be concerned with natural, not historical, objects, and its methods are considered to be those of natural science, not those of history. Psychology is committed to investigating processes like cognition, perception, and motivation, as historically invariant phenomena of nature, not as historically determined social phenomena.
>
> (Danziger, 1997, p. 9)

Its "wishful identification with the natural sciences" (Danziger, 1997, p. 9) led psychologists to believe that the proper unit of analysis was a "natural" object. In this way psychology "solved" what Vygotsky identified as its insoluble methodological contradiction of being a natural science of unnatural things. And so psychology became about human beings in the ways that zoology is about animal life, physics is about matter and astronomy is about stars. With apparent ease psychology thus dismissed that which is most fascinating and significant about being human – our subjectivity (historicalness, socialness, consciousness and self-reflexivity) – to apply research methods constructed to investigate objects that do not have these qualities.

As subjectivity and consciousness faded from consideration, psychology found the ideal candidate for its object of scientific study in behavior. According to Danziger, this new psychological category was key to establishing the legitimacy of the discipline. Behavior unified psychology, providing the common "scientific" laws and the common discourse that made it possible for psychology to claim the existence of phenomena important to and belonging to all fields of psychology.

Behaviour became the category that Psychology would use to define its subject matter: Whether one was trying to explain a child's answers on a problem-solving task, an adult's neurotic symptomotology, or a white rat's reaction to finding itself in a laboratory maze, one was ultimately trying to explain the same thing, namely, the behaviour of an organism. Classifying such diverse phenomena together as instances of "behaviour" was the first necessary step in establishing the claim that Psychology was one science with one set of explanatory principles.

(Danziger, 1997, p. 86)

Behavior met the criteria necessary for a unit of analysis of the new discipline fashioning itself after the natural and physical sciences. It was the kind of phenomenon that could be measured and quantified, that could be "found" over and over again and proclaimed the unifying factor for all the varied things human beings do. And so, psychology became the study of behavior, identified as a naturally occurring psychological category.

As the great unifier, behavior came to be what psychologists (and ordinary people) see. Psychologists of our day seek to discover the psychological foundations of violence and aggression in order to gain insight into and reverse the tide of the increase in *violent and aggressive behavior*; the widespread use and often devastating effects of drugs have shaped a billion dollar addiction industry in the USA which includes the psychological study of *addictive behavior*; the information highway challenges psychologists to rethink *learning behavior*; the pressure of identity politics made clear the need for intensified study of variations in the *communicative behavior* of various groups as compared along gender, race, ethnic and class lines, and so on.

As the unit of study for psychology, however, behavior leaves a lot to be desired. It ignores the socio-cultural-historicalness of individuals and groups of people. It obscures the continuously emergent and dialectical activity of human life, and denies that human beings are simultaneously agents and products (tools-and-results) of qualitative change. Behavior relates to human beings as unchanging in character in spite of everyday and scientific evidence to the contrary, namely, that we undergo fundamental, qualitative transformations in our character and, yet, we "remain" human beings.

Identifying behavior as the subject matter of psychology, the basic unit of analysis no matter what, where, when, how or who, has had significant social, cultural and political consequences. It accounts, in large part, for the conservatism of psychology as an approach to understanding human life. Understanding human beings as essentially, fundamentally and naturally a *behaving species* is an acceptance of alienation as a universal human condition. I am using "alienation" as Marx did to refer to the separation of the products of production from the process of their production, that is, as commodities.[9] Alienation in this sense is not limited to cars and loaves of bread, but is the normal way of seeing and relating in contemporary Western culture. Behavior is the perfect unit of analysis for a culture dominated by alienation, a culture in which the process of production, not only of material goods but of human experience of all kinds, is separated from its "products" which are then reified (as "natural") and commodified (as behavior). Scientific psychology, in this way, produces a limited research strategy for discovering and creating anything transformative about human life. Behavior is a particular human-social phenomenon produced under definite social-historical-cultural conditions, not "the constant," not the meta-category, but a variable. It is no more "natural" to human beings than surfing the Net, hitchhiking or undergoing open heart surgery (see Newman and Holzman, 1996/2006 and 1997 for fuller discussion of alienation).

ACTIVITY

Activity is one alternative to behavior. While Vygotsky never abandoned the term behavior, it seems clear from both his meta-psychological (methodological) and psychological writings that he did not mean by it the ahistorical, asocial, acultural motion or actions of particulars. In his search to shed light on the historical development of human beings and human culture (which were, to him, inseparable elements of a totality), the question of what development is and how to conceptualize it was critical. How does a child get from "here" to "there?" If development is a continuous process, how is it that it appears periodically to stop? If human culture is collectively produced, is individual experience an illusion?

Vygotsky found in Marx the concept of activity, which he adapted and expanded upon. To understand Marx's conception of activity it is essential to recognize that, for Marx, human beings are social beings. He did not set the individual in opposition to society, as can be seen in this remark: "It is above all necessary to avoid postulating 'society' once again as an abstraction confronting the individual. The individual *is* the *social being*" (Marx, 1967, p. 130). But from this statement, two directions of emphasis emerge in Marx's thinking and writing. Marx the philosopher goes one way – toward a radical social-cultural-historical humanism (not to be confused with the humanist tradition that glorifies individualism) – and Marx the economist-sociologist goes another – toward a paradigmatic materialism. (The latter is the more familiar Marx of political science and philosophy texts.)

For the philosopher – the methodological Marx of his earlier writings – activity was the social, dialectical, revolutionary character of human life, as these excerpts indicate: "The coincidence of the changing of circumstances and of human activity or self-changing can be conceived and rationally understood only as *revolutionary practice*" (Marx, 1974, p. 121); and "*As* society itself produces *man* as *man*, so it is *produced* by him. Activity and mind are social in their content as well as in their *origin*; they are *social* activity and *social* mind" (Marx, 1967, p. 129). Thus, for Marx activity is fundamentally social, communal, reflexive and reconstructive – it is human beings exercising their power as "activity-ists," that is, as transformers of totalities (themselves and their environments). Unlike most of his followers, not to mention most psychologists, Marx saw no wall between the subjective and the socio-cultural. The transformation of the world and of ourselves as human beings was one and the same revolutionary task.

In his later economic writings and in his collaborations with Engels, Marx de-emphasized the revolutionary and dialectical quality of activity in favor of a (some would say vulgar) materialist emphasis on the role of labor in historically transforming human behavior and consciousness. It is through human labor and the use of tools that human beings master nature and in the process transform themselves.

Vygotsky brought Marx's conception of activity to his meta-theoretical studies of psychology and his investigations of learning and development in childhood, and thinking, speaking, play and imagination more broadly. (Vygotsky was also greatly influenced by Hegel and Engels.) And, as with Marx, two directions of emphasis emerge in Vygotsky's thinking and writing. The methodological

Vygotsky followed the methodological Marx. "Social activity and social mind" inspired Vygotsky toward seeing the unit of analysis for the nondualistic psychology he was so eager to create, a psychology that – unlike behaviorism, introspection or psycho-analysis – recognized the unity of consciousness and action and denied the separation of the objective and the subjective. Social in both content and origin, activity is a cultural-historical phenom-enon that emerges and transforms along with transformations in economic and cultural production. It is how human beings trans-form the existing circumstances, develop as individuals and as a species, and create culture. Activity – the ordinary person's "search for method" – is the human capacity to make tools-and-results.

Along with this radical statement of *tool (-and-result) making* as the dialectical process of human development, Vygotsky also wrote a great deal about *tool use*, especially the role of psychological tools in human development. In this, he followed the later Marx and Engels, and associated activity with the historical process of human beings actively transforming the world through labor, and the accompanying emergence of language and consciousness. The symbol systems, tools and structures of collective activity are what make us human, i.e. socio-cultural-historical. Vygotsky identified learning and development in early childhood largely in terms of the processes by which language and other psychological tools come to be incorporated and used.

Vygotsky's work is considered foundational to the international school of thought known as activity theory. It is generally accepted that activity theory originated in the early years of the Soviet Union as a psychology based in Marxist principles. As advanced by colleagues after his death in 1934, most particularly, A. L. Leontiev, activity theory took the "tool-user" turn rather than the "tool-and-result maker" turn, and this is what dominates today – even as the term activity theory is no longer reserved for Marxist, Soviet or Russian-style psychology but rather encompasses an array of socio-cultural and cultural-historical perspectives. (It should be noted, however, that some scholars in the field vigor-ously debate the origins, history and current status of activity theory relative to other Soviet and Western traditions, with the usual territorial and definitional tensions that accompany such debate; see Repkin, 2003; Robbins and Stetsenko, 2002; Wertsch, 1981.) In most contemporary work carried out by activity-theoretic psychologists, educational researchers and others, activity is understood as the specifically human form of socio-historically produced behaviors that are motivated by (similarly socio-historically produced) needs and goals, mediated by (similarly socio-culturally produced) tools, such as language and other artifacts, and through which culture is produced and reproduced.

By infusing activity with *mediation* and *motivation* these researchers are back in the trap Vygotsky was trying to escape – the trap of a dualistically divided world of objective reality and subjective experience. For if cultural tools (most notably, language) mediate our relationship to nature, ourselves and other people, then there must exist a distance between persons and the world, which makes it necessary for something to serve as a connecting link or mediator. Learning and development, in this view, become the use of these tools to appropriate the existing culture and acquire knowledge of the world. And what can account for this knowledge-seeking behavior? The answer? – motivation and culturally produced needs and goals. The cognitive–emotive split of psychology is intact. Vygotsky's methodological challenge to it, his recognition of the seduction of psychology's cognitive bias, his radical stance toward method, his application of Marx's revolutionary dialectics to human development are gone. And with their elimination, his body of work is reduced to a *theory of mind*.

BEING AND BECOMING

I see Vygotsky's work very differently. Not as a theory of mind, but as a *theory of becoming*. To the extent that he ever settled on a conceptualization of development, it had to do with the qualitative transformation of totalities. It had to do with the process of becoming and not with the state of being. Activity provides the foundation to move psychology from the study of "what is" to the study of "what is becoming" (which entails "what is"). Vygotsky's attempt to create a dialectical conception of human development (the activity of becoming) and a dialectical methodology for studying it (tool-and-result) reframes the question of human development in such a way as to embrace its paradoxical nature: How can something be both what it is and what it is not? His analysis of children's learning and development, while not a complete explication of this phenomenon, provides some methodological insight with which to tackle it.

Vygotsky broke through the linear and causal understandings of learning (and/or instruction) and development and how they are related. His writings extensively present and argue against the prevailing views that learning depends on and follows development or that learning and development are related in some unspecified manner. ["Instruction is not limited to trailing after development or moving stride for stride along with it. It can move ahead of development, pushing it further and eliciting new formations" (Vygotsky, 1987, p. 198).] He conceptualized learning and development not as discrete particulars that interact, but as a dialectical unity in which learning leads development (Vygotsky, 1987).[10]

Newman and I came to understand "learning leading development" as an important advance in bringing Marx's dialectical conception of activity to psychology (Newman and Holzman, 1993). In Vygotsky's descriptions of how very young children become speakers of a language, for example, Newman and I see something other than the mastering of a mediational means of acquiring knowledge about the world (that is, using an instrumental tool). What we see is the creating of a developmental environment and development – simultaneously (that is, making a tool-and-result). We see a glimpse of what the dialectical process of being/becoming looks like – how young children are related to simultaneously as who they are and who they are not (who they are becoming), and that this is how they develop. With their caretakers young children create developmental environments that support them to do what is beyond them, to be who they are becoming even as they are who they are. They speak before they know how to and their creative imitation of the language spoken to and around them is fully accepted. The process of learning and the product of learning are created together. Through their joint activity, young children and their caretakers, siblings, etc., create environments for learning leading development and, in the practice of that dialectical activity, they create the unity, learning and developing.

How do they do it? Vygotsky describes it as being a head taller than you are (Vygotsky, 1978, p. 102). Newman and I call it performing in the theatrical sense of the word (Newman and Holzman, 1996/2006, 1997). This kind of performing has similarities to the pretend play of early childhood in which children are doing what is familiar to them and, at the same time, doing things that are brand new, things that are beyond them. And they do this all day long. We let very young children perform ahead of themselves – speaking, drawing pictures, reading books (and much more) before they know how. This performing kind of play and these spaces for performance are essential to development and learning – not only in early childhood but for all of us at all ages.

Development, in this understanding, is the activity of creating who you are by performing who you are not. It is an ensemble – not a solo – performance. And Vygotsky's zone of proximal development is not a zone at all, or a societal scaffold, but an activity – simultaneously the performance space and the performance (Holzman, 1997a; Newman and Holzman, 1993).

This is a brief and incomplete summary of the Vygotsky who has emerged through my own struggles to understand and break free of the constraining concepts and language of paradigmatic psychology. In the chapters that follow I unpack what I have said so far through introducing several practices and programs conducted by colleagues of mine and sharing my understanding of Vygotsky's presence in them. Which brings us back to the issues of paradigms, paradigm shifts and the cognitive bias. Earlier I said that my concern was not to effect a paradigm shift but a shift away from paradigmism. Yet, isn't what I have presented another paradigm?

Yes and no. Yes, if making and transforming paradigms is inseparable from the *nonparadigmatic activity* of groupings of people creating new forms and performances of life. If new ways of seeing emerge with new ways of being. This, however, is not how paradigms and paradigm shifts are typically understood. A paradigm is, after all, cognitive. It prioritizes thought over action. It is, in effect, a guide to action. It is a very sophisticated form of tool for result.

The ability to use tools, both physical and psychological, for instrumental purposes was a magnificent scientific discovery and human development. Navigation and world exploration (and accompanying exploitation), mass production and industrial capitalism, disease identification and life-saving medical advances, Descartes' cogito, the institutionalization of learning, the steam engine, electricity, automobiles, airplanes, space travel, Gestalt psychology, psychoanalysis, Piagetian theory, cybernetics – the list of accomplishments from the late sixteenth to mid twentieth century is endless. But harkening back to Marx, human activity and human mind are social phenomena that develop under definite historical conditions. Remembering Danziger, discovery and its discourse is always historically situated. Rephrasing Vygotsky, the Scientific

Revolution solved certain tasks raised by history. It also created other tasks, which, in this first decade of the twenty-first century, have proven unsolvable with its instrumental tools.

Vygotsky surely did not put forth a nonparadigmatic view of doing science. He did, however, recognize that human beings do – and must do – more than use existing tools, make new instrumental tools and acquire knowledge. He discovered that human beings also do dialectics – reshaping the very environments that determine them, performing who they are becoming, creating culture and transforming the world. The "products" of this activity are not outcomes, but part of the unity that is "process-and-product" or tool-and-result.

Chapter 2

Vygotsky in therapy

Creating zones of emotional development

> What is under consideration is not the ontological state of affairs, but the ontological commitments of a discourse. What there *is* does not in general depend on one's use of language, but what one *says* there is does.
>
> (W. V. O. Quine, *From a Logical Point of View*, emphasis added, 1961, p. 103)

My desire to understand what language is and how it works is what led me to study psychology. My desire to change the world is what led me to study psychotherapy. Bringing the two together transformed how I understood both.

I came to psychology already cognitively biased. Emotionality wasn't something that I thought or read about and no one I knew growing up or as a young adult had any experience in psychotherapy (that I was aware of). When I did learn a little about it in college, my disinterest only increased, for its premise – that an explanation or interpretation for how you were feeling could change how you were feeling – made no sense to me. Furthermore, my undergraduate studies in English and literature, and my graduate training in linguistics and developmental psychology, treated speaking, problem solving, reading and writing as cognitive tasks. Not explicitly taught, the cognitive–emotive divide was part of the hidden curriculum of my education.

It was a lecture on the topic of Marxism and mental illness that sparked my interest in emotions. Fred Newman, the speaker, was as skeptical as I was about psychotherapy but, unlike me, he had done a lot of thinking about it and had first-hand experience. Newman drew many connections between psychotherapy and politics as he sprinkled his talk with analyses of economics, capitalism, the ego, the working class, science, ideology, the mind and language, and presented ideas of Marx, Freud, Skinner and contemporary thinkers like Chomsky and Goffman. I was intrigued.

As Newman and I began to work together I learned the source of his criticism of psychotherapy and how the social therapy he was developing responded to that criticism and was a part of his political activism. In the beginning, social therapy was a 1960s-style radical therapy, radical in its explicit politics – in its understandings that living under capitalism makes people emotionally "sick" and that therapy could be a tool in the service of progressive politics. Like other radical therapies of the time (e.g. antipsychiatry, feminist, gay, antiracist), social therapy engaged the authoritarian sexism, racism, classism and homophobia of traditional psychotherapy.

But social therapy was radical philosophically and scientifically as well as politically. Newman's political motivation may have been social therapy's reason for being, but his studies of philosophy of science and of language, and foundations of mathematics (and later, of Marxian dialectics) were the roots of its growth. He rejected therapy's premises and major conceptions – explanation, interpretation, the notion of an inner self that therapists and clients needed to delve into, and other dualistic and otherwise problematic conceptions. At the same time, he had gone into therapy in the late 1960s and found it extremely helpful. As he tells the story, the experience forced him to deal with the contradiction that this activity, which he believed to be based on faulty premises, actually worked (Newman, 1999). He did not believe in an inner life and yet found that doing therapy, in which talking about your inner life is what you do, was helpful to him. Not willing to concede to its existence, he wondered how this could be. Without having anything that would count as an answer, Newman began a therapy practice in which he tried to help people with whatever emotional pain they were experiencing, without invoking the conception of an inner self which he was supposed to help them get more deeply into, without diagnosing their problem, analyzing their childhood, or interpreting their current life.

Along with rejecting the concept of inner life, Newman critiqued the individualistic bias of Western culture (including its economics, psychology and psychotherapy) from philosophical and Marxist perspectives, in particular, the conceptions of totality and the particular. To Newman's understanding, in creating and glorifying the isolated individual, psychology adopted the philosophical belief that particulars are what is "real" and that totalities are an abstraction. The notion that emotions are the mental states of isolated individuals is a version of this misconception of the stuff of the world, one that Newman believed was a major source of people's emotional pain (Newman and Holzman, 1996/2006). Helping people therapeutically, therefore, meant challenging them to relate to emotions as other than private mental states and to themselves as other than "particulars." A group therapeutic modality was potentially an environment more conducive to this kind of challenging than was one-on-one (individual) therapy. Group was the starting point, and has remained the primary organization of social therapy for more than 30 years.

In most group therapies, the group serves as a context for the therapist to help individuals with their emotional problems. In social therapy, the group – not its individual members – is the therapeutic unit. Clients who come together to form a social therapy group are given a task – to create their group as an environment in which they can get help. This emphasis on *group activity* is a collective, practical challenge to the assumption that the way people get help therapeutically is to relate to themselves and be related to by others as individuals, complete with problems and with inner selves. It is in groups that a person's felt experience of being the center of the universe (that nothing else is going on in the world except how one is feeling) can be most effectively challenged.[1]

I began to work formally with Newman and about a dozen others, a combination of social workers, community activists and social science graduate students, in establishing an independent therapy, research and training center. In 1979 we opened the New York Institute for Social Therapy and Research (dropping "New York" from the name a few years later). For the next 10 years, this organization served as incubator for numerous experimental projects and activities that brought the fledgling methodological approach of social therapy and a progressive political agenda to bear on schooling and its failing learning model, the under-development of inner-city youth, and the nature and function of culture, especially theatre. These projects gradually developed their own institutional identities and became legally and financially separate from each other. The institute that spawned them transformed into a nonprofit research and training center, the East Side Institute for Group and Short Term Psychotherapy. All currently continue to work together as part of an expanding national and international development community.[2]

The Vygotsky I brought with me to the study and advancement of social therapy and to the building of these projects and organizations was that of *Mind in Society*, the collection of excerpts from his writings compiled by Cole, John-Steiner, Scribner, and Souberman and published in 1978 (Vygotsky, 1978). As history has played out, it was this slim volume that awakened psychologists and educators, if not to Vygotsky's revolutionary scientific genius, then at least to pay him some attention. This was the Vygotsky embodied in the title – minds and the processes and functions presumed to be carried out "in" them (conceptualizing, problem solving, thinking, speaking, imagining, and so on) are social phenomena. Developed through human history in ways specific to each epoch and culture, for each person these higher psychological processes originate "interpsychologically," that is, socially, through the activities people engage in. They become "intrapsychological," that is, part of a person's repertoire of capacities, skills and experiences, by virtue of these social interactions.

This was also a cognitively overdetermined Vygotsky. The book contains no writings on emotions or bridging the cognitive–emotive divide, and the editors equate higher psychological processes with cognition. For example, in describing Vygotsky's view of what distinguishes humans from animals, John-Steiner and Souberman state: "In the development of higher functions – that is, in the internalization of the processes of knowing – the particulars of human social existence are reflected in human cognition" (John-Steiner and Souberman, 1978, p. 132). Vygotsky's work was clearly taken as an excitingly new cognitive theory. I do not mean this as a criticism of the book or its editors – who were immersed in their own studies critical of mainstream approaches to cognition and learning at the time – but rather to historically locate points in Vygotsky's growing popularity and in my Vygotskian journey. This journey includes the innovative work of Cole's Laboratory of Comparative Human Cognition at the Rockefeller University, which I was part of from 1976 to 1979. The lab seized on Vygotsky's nondualistic conception of learning and development as socio-cultural in support of a new theory of cognition. His attempt to "de-dualize" cognition and emotion was not noticed.

Uncomfortable with the splits between inside and outside, psychological and social, and child and environment that were foundational for conducting psychological research, I was enthusiastic about Vygotsky's formulations and where the Rockefeller laboratory took them. The major issue we were confronting was the validity of the experimental method of cognitive psychology (Cole, Hood and McDermott, 1978). If psychological theory and findings are generated in the laboratory (or under experimental conditions designed to replicate the laboratory), how can they be generalized to everyday life? In other words, did they have any "ecological validity" and, if not, could we develop a methodology for a psychology that *was* ecologically valid? (For a discussion of the problem of ecological validity and the role of the Rockefeller University research in the overall agenda of cultural psychology, see Cole, 1996, Chapter 8, especially pp. 222–258.)

We considered the laboratory as a methodology and not merely a physical location. It seemed to us that naturalistic and observational research conducted in everyday life settings was guided as much by the laboratory's methodological assumptions as any research conducted inside a psych lab. Conversely, much of what happens inside the laboratory during an experiment is what happens everywhere – but in the lab it is ignored because the experimental paradigm disallows it. We hoped our research would not only expose the pervasive laboratory biases in how children's learning and development were studied and understood, but also help us create a new, ecologically valid set of investigative practices. This was our "search for method." Ultimately, our goal was to impact positively on the inequality and inadequacy of American schooling.

In one project we observed and interacted with 8- to 10-year-old children in a variety of school and nonschool settings in order to see how cognitive acts – for example, remembering, problem solving, reading, reasoning and so on – were alike and different in the different settings. When I talked to "regular people" about the project, I said we wanted to find out some things about "how come kids who are street smart are school dumb." When we observed children in nonschool settings, we saw few instances of school- or test-like acts and virtually none carried out by an individual child; there was an "invisibility of cognitive tasks" (Cole, 1996, p. 246). Outside of school, children solved problems and remembered things together, not in isolation from each other. When we looked at children who were having problems in school, we did not see their cognitive or emotional difficulties. Instead, we saw a complex, socially constructed cultural scene involving many people and institutions. We were finding evidence for the "interpsychological-ness" of higher psychological processes in middle childhood. Cognition, we concluded, is a social and cultural achievement that occurs through a process of people collectively constructing environments in which to act on the world. It is located not in an individual's head, but in the "person–environment interface" (Cole, Hood and McDermott, 1978). Learning disability, we con-cluded, does not exist outside of or separate from the interactive work or joint activity that people do which, intentionally or not, creates "displays" of disability (Hood, McDermott and Cole, 1980; McDermott and Hood, 1982). An ecologically valid psychology would have to take this method, and these findings and conclusions, into account. (See also Cole, 1996 for discussion of this research.)[3]

This notion of *people collectively constructing environments in which to act on the world*, discovered through a reading of Vygotsky as cognitive psychologist and an application/advancement of his ideas to cognitive psychology, was something I brought to the topics of psychotherapy and emotionality through the study of social therapeutic practice. My journey to the unity of cognition and emotion had to pass through the zone of proximal development.

VYGOTSKY'S ZONE OF PROXIMAL DEVELOPMENT AND SOCIAL THERAPY'S ZONE OF EMOTIONAL DEVELOPMENT

Vygotsky's zone of proximal development (shortened to 'zpd' in the USA and 'zoped' elsewhere),[4] contemporary Vygotskians would agree, is an environment in which to act on the world. The question is, how *collectively constructed* is it?

Vygotsky invoked the concept of the zpd in putting forth his view that learning and development are a dialectical unity in which learning does not follow but leads development (Vygotsky, 1978, 1987). The zpd played a key role in his refutation of the dominant perspective that learning follows and is dependent upon develop-ment and in his related criticism of traditional instructional and assessment practices ("Instruction would be completely unneces-sary if it merely utilized what had already matured in the develop-mental process, if it were not itself a source of development," Vygotsky, 1987, p. 212). In addition, the zpd was the occasion for

Vygotsky to take a fresh view of imitation and its role in learning and development.

Even so, contemporary Vygotskians sometimes argue over the precise context in which Vygotsky introduced the zpd and what he meant by it. While this kind of debate is common among scholars in all fields, especially when particular writings become available at different times, in Vygotsky's case there is the added factor of multiple translations of the same work, with significant differences among them. In an essay historically situating certain of Vygotsky's ideas, Glick points out how English-language volumes of Vygotsky's work published at different times present a different Vygotsky – and a different zpd (Glick, 2004). No doubt this plays a role in the varying understandings of the zpd and their accompanying research agendas.

One way to understand the zpd is as a characteristic or property of an individual child. This understanding stems from passages like the following:

> The psychologist must not limit his analysis to functions that have matured. He must consider those that are in the process of maturing. If he is to fully evaluate the state of the child's development, the psychologist must consider not only the actual level of development but *the zone of proximal development*.
> (Vygotsky, 1987, pp. 208–209, original emphasis)

Some educational researchers who have interpreted this statement in terms of assessment (that is, that the zpd is or produces a measure of a child's potential) have been inspired by Vygotsky to devise alternative means of measuring and evaluating individual children (for example, Allal and Pelgrims, 2000; Lantoff, 2000; Lidz and Gindis, 2003; Newman, Griffin and Cole, 1989; Tharp and Gallimore, 1988).

In other passages Vygotsky wrote of the zpd as part of his argument for the socialness of the "learning-leading-development" process and the role of joint activity and collaboration in the child's life, as in the following passage:

> What we call the Zone of Proximal Development . . . is the distance between the actual developmental level as determined by independent problem solving, and the level of potential

development as determined through problem solving under guidance or in collaboration with more capable peers.

(Vygotsky, 1978, p. 86)

The mention of those "more capable" in this description inspired some psychologists to reconceptualize the zpd as some form of aid, termed prosthesis (by Shotter, 1989 and Wertsch, 1991) and scaffolding (by Wood, Bruner and Ross, 1976). The idea has caught on, so much so that the typical college textbook equates the zpd with scaffolding and attributes both terms to Vygotsky (for example, Berk and Winsler, 1995; MacNaughton and Williams, 1998; Wood and Attfield, 1996). Additionally, most educational research with this perspective (and there is a lot of it) takes "the aid" to be a single, more capable individual, most often an adult (termed "expert" in contrast to the "novice" child). This is despite Vygotsky's use of the word "peers."

Similarly, in the following oft-quoted passage, it is common for "social level" and "interpsychological" to be reduced to a two-person unit:

Every function in the child's cultural development appears twice: first on the social level and later, on the individual level; first *between* people *(interpsychological)*, and then *inside* the child *(intrapsychological)*. This applies equally to all voluntary attention, to logical memory, and to the formation of concepts. All the higher mental functions originate as actual relations between people.

(Vygotsky, 1978, p. 57, original emphasis)

In other places Vygotsky emphasized that the socialness of learning and development is collective; that the zpd is not exclusively or even primarily a dyadic relationship, and that what is key to the zpd is that people are doing something together. For example, "Learning awakens a variety of internal developmental processes that are able to operate only when the child is interacting with people in his environment and in cooperation with his peers" (Vygotsky, 1978, p. 90; see also Vygotsky, 1994a).

The necessity of collective activity for learning-leading-development is at the forefront of Vygotsky's approach to special education. His writings on this subject (collected and published in English as *Fundamentals of Defectology*, 1993) argue that development should not be written off for children with abnormalities such as retardation, blindness or deafness, nor should these children be segregated and placed in schools with only children like themselves. Vygotsky made the point that qualitative transformation (as opposed to rote learning) is a collective accomplishment – a "collective form of 'working together'" he called it in an essay entitled, "The collective as a factor in the development of the abnormal child" (Vygotsky, 2004a, p. 202). In this same essay he characterized the social, or interpsychological, level of development (in the quote above) as "a function of collective behavior, as a form of cooperation or cooperative activity" (p. 202).

This idea of the zpd as a "collective form of working together" opens up the theoretical significance and practical applicability of Vygotsky's concept considerably. Vygotsky seems to be saying that learning-leading-development is *created collectively*. This suggests that the zpd is more usefully understood as a process than as a spatio-temporal entity, an activity rather than an actual zone, space or distance. In the terms presented in Chapter 1, for me, the zpd is dialectical, tool-and-result activity, simultaneously the creating of the zone (environment) and what is created (learning-leading-development). This new understanding of a developmental way of working together, my coworkers and I believed, should not be confined to either cognitive tasks or early and middle childhood, but had broad implications across settings and the life span.

Yet with most contemporary work in the Vygotskian tradition, the zpd is taken to be a dyadic relationship of assisting rather than the collective activity of creating. Among the complexity of factors producing this difference between us, that I look at the zpd from a therapeutic perspective and a group therapy location seems to me a significant one.[5] As an insider to social therapy, both participant and investigator, I could not ignore emotionality or easily impose a cognitive spin on what was going on in the therapy groups. I learned how to see without the imposition of psychology's cognitive–emotive divide. As a developmental psychologist informed by Marx and Newman, what I saw in social therapy was groupings of people collectively working together and creating the "emotional zone" that *is* their new emotionality (their learning-leading-development). I doubt if this activity is "seeable" in a classroom or other settings organized for the acquisition of knowledge. (As I will discuss in Chapter 4, seeing the emotional zpd at work in social therapy was very important when I turned to a re-examination of the zpd in educational settings.)

The collective creating of the zpd points to the dialectic of human life (being/becoming) in that it entails relating to people as capable of doing what they do not yet know how to do and what is, therefore, beyond them (similar to what Vygotsky described as "the child's potential to move from what he is able to do to what he is not," Vygotsky, 1987, p. 212). Vygotsky described some of how this looks for very young children and for children with disabilities. I see an analogous process in social therapy groups. In both cases, ordinary people employ a creative methodology of producing environments in which and how they organize and reorganize their relationships to themselves, each other and to the tools (both material and psychological) and objects of their world. They construct "zones" that allow them *to become*. (In the case of children and their caregivers it is done without conscious effort, while in therapy groups it takes considerable conscious effort.)

CREATIVE IMITATION AND PERFORMANCE

According to Vygotsky, "A full understanding of the concept of the zone of proximal development must result in a reevaluation of the role of imitation in learning" (1978, p. 87). He discounted the mechanical view of imitation that was "rooted in traditional psychology, as well as in everyday consciousness" and the individualistically biased inferences drawn from it, for example, that "the child can imitate anything" and that "what I can do by imitating says nothing about my own mind" (1987, p. 209). To him, imitation was an active, creative and fundamentally social process that was essential to creating the zpd. Children do not imitate anything and everything as a parrot does, but rather what is beyond them in their environment/relationships. In the language I have been using, *creatively imitating* others in their daily inter-actions – saying what someone else says, moving to music, picking up a pencil and "writing" – is relating to oneself as/being related to by others as/performing as a speaker, a dancer, a writer, a learner, a human being. It is how children are capable of doing so much in collective activity.

Vygotsky's analysis of the language-learning zpd (in *Thinking and Speech*) can serve as an excellent illustration of creative imitation at work. He showed that babies and toddlers do not learn language or are taught language in the cognitive, acquisitional and transmittal sense typical of institutionalized learning and teaching. They develop as speakers, language makers and language users as an inseparable part of joining and transforming the social life of their family (community, group). When babies begin to babble they are speaking before they know how by virtue of the speakers around them creating conversation with them. Mothers, fathers, grandparents, siblings and others neither tell babies that they are too young, correct them, give them a grammar book and diction-ary to study, nor remain silent around them. Rather, they relate to infants and babies as capable of far more than they could possibly do "naturally." They relate to them as fellow speakers, feelers, thinkers and makers of meaning. This is what makes it possible for very young children to do what they are not yet capable of. The babbling baby's rudimentary speech is a *creative imitation* of the more developed speaker's speech. At the same time, the more developed speakers "complete" the baby, and the "conversation" continues.

I see creative imitation as a type of performance. When they are playing with language in this way in the language-learning zpd, babies are simultaneously performing – *becoming* – themselves. In the theatrical sense of the word, performing is a way of taking "who we are" and creating something new – in this case a newly emerging speaker, on the stage a newly emerging character – through incorporating "the other." The capacity to speak and to make meaning is inextricably connected to transforming the total environment (a socio-cultural form of life) of speakers in the activity of performing an ordinary "unnatural" act.[6]

While linking creative imitation with performance, and performance with the dialectic being/becoming that is development, may seem at first glance to be far from Vygotsky's work, its roots are there in his writings. For me, the inspiration initially came from his discussions of children's play (Vygotsky, 1978, pp. 92–104) in which he noted that the zpd of play creates situations in which "a child's greatest achievements are possible, achievements that tomorrow will become her basic level of real action and morality" (Vygotsky, 1978, p. 102). In addition, Vygotsky brought the subject of play to bear on many topics, including thinking and speaking, school instruction, and the development of imagination, concepts, memory and personality.

An essay published in English in Volume 4 of his collected works ("Conclusion; further research; development of personality and world view in the child," Vygotsky, 1997b) is particularly relevant to what I am saying about performance and development. Linking early childhood play to the formation of personality and world-view, Vygotsky wrote that the preschool child "can be somebody else just as easily as he can be himself" (p. 249). Vygotsky attributed this to the child's lack of recognition that she or he is an "I" and went on to discuss how personality and play transform through later childhood. While Vygotsky gave no indication that there might be a downside to these transformations, his astute observation of the young child's *performance ability* has been made use of in social therapy and the ongoing development of a psychology of becoming.

As I understand it, the downside in our culture is that as children perform their way into cultural and societal adaptation, their potential for continuous development becomes limited. What they have learned through performing becomes routinized and rigidified. By middle school (which, in only rare instances, is a zpd), many children have become so skilled at acting out certain roles that they no longer keep creating new performances of themselves (that is, developing). By the time they are adults, most people have an identity as "this kind of person" – someone who does certain things (and does them in certain ways) and feels certain ways. Anything other than that would not be "true" to "who *I* am." This is the identity that people bring into therapy.

Over years of studying social therapeutic practice, I have come to see it as a radical building upon Vygotsky's observation about young children's performance ability. Performing as someone else (being oneself and other than oneself) is the source of development – for Vygotsky, at the time of life before "I" and its culturally produced fixed identity; for Newman, throughout the life course. Social therapeutic methodology has evolved into a conscious effort to revitalize this human capacity, and that is, in large part, how I understand its effectiveness.

The theatre itself was another source of relating to people in therapy and, indeed, all people everywhere, as ensemble performers of their lives. In the mid 1980s, Newman began to write and direct plays in addition to practicing social therapy. He found the work of creating a play developmental for everyone involved, sparking an interest in exploring the relationship between therapy and theatre, particularly the relationship between his clients taking on the task of creating their groups and what actors do when creating an ensemble on the stage. Two East Side Institute social therapy weekend retreats gave him the opportunity to experiment with ways to unite theatre and therapy. Newman titled the first one, "The Play is the Therapy: Emotional Growth Through Performance." The 200 or so people (a mix of helping professionals and clients) took part in a series of improvisational performance workshops, sometimes working together as a whole and at other times in smaller groups creating separate skits. The weekend culminated in the production of a sprawling improvisational comedy. At the second retreat 6 months later, Newman asked participants to do 1-minute performances of their lives. After each of these performances, Newman and a colleague gave directorial suggestions and asked each participant to perform for 30 more seconds in response to that suggestion. Based on these performances of a lifetime and the performance personas they projected, combinations of people got together and worked on improvisational situations. Once again, the weekend ended with the ensemble putting on an improvisational play. The 1-minute performances became the signature exercise of the theatre-based executive education consulting firm I discuss in Chapter 5, named appropriately, Performance of a Lifetime.

One after another, the participants said that the experience was very therapeutic. Newman also felt that this activity, focused entirely on creative theatrical process, was emotionally developmental in the way that he believed therapy should be. Creating environments (stages) for ordinary adults to perform – an activity sanctioned in our culture only for very young children and professional actors – gave them the opportunity to discover that they *could* perform. This "aha" was a new activity; neither cognitive nor emotional, it was therapeutic in the social therapeutic sense.

Since then, performance has come to center stage, methodologically speaking, in social therapy. On Newman's part, he has come to relate to therapy sessions as therapy plays, and clients as an ensemble of performers who, with the therapist's help, are staging a new therapy play each session, and experiencing themselves as the collective creators of their emotional growth (Holzman and Mendez, 2003; Newman, 1996).[7] Additionally, the two of us have helped colleagues develop educational and cultural projects for young people and adults that advance a performance (rather than a cognitive) model of learning. I will be discussing some of these projects in later chapters.

It is speculated that some time probably less than one million years ago, our ancestors – not yet *Homo sapiens* – stood up. It is also speculated that some time probably less than 100,000 years ago, our ancestors – now *Homo erectus* – evolved a brain structure and size making them capable of cognitive feats worthy of the modern attribution "sapien" (wisdom). Nearly all that human beings have accomplished is generally understood to derive from, evolutionarily speaking, these two qualitative transformations. About the first, our "upright posture," I have little to say. It is the second, our "epistemic posture," if you will, and, even more, our epistemic *posturing* (cognitive bias) that social therapeutic methodology challenges.

Epistemic refers to knowledge. Epistemic posture refers to the importance of the uniquely human ability to pursue and amass knowledge. By epistemic posturing I mean the glorification of this ability and the way its product, knowledge, plays an authoritarian role in the contemporary world. "I think therefore I am" should not be taken as a universal truth for all time (past, present and future), but as a culturally and historically situated belief. Might it have outlived its applicability and usefulness? I believe it has. Influenced by Vygotsky's search for method and synthesizing our different orientations, Newman and I have come to see perform-ance as a new ontology, both the process and the product of human development. People are primarily performers, not thinkers or knowers.

INDIVIDUALS AND GROUPS

As I have said, social therapy is a group therapy. This is the case even for "individual" sessions, which are, after all, groups of two. Typically, clients who come to social therapy will work in this group of two for awhile and then go into what is more easily recognizable as a group. These groups are typically comprised of 10 to 25 people, a mix of women and men of varying ages, ethnicities, sexual orien-tations, class backgrounds and economic status, professions and "presenting problems." The groups are heterogeneous because in that kind of environment people's notion of a fixed identity can be challenged, whether it be an identity based on gender, ethnicity or other category, a diagnostic label, or, simply, "That's the kind of person I am." Moreover, the more diverse the elements, the more material there is with which to create. Most groups are ongoing (although social therapists periodically do time-limited groups) and meet weekly for 90 minutes. Some group members remain for years, others months; people leave and new members join. The elements of the therapeutic zpd are thus continuously changing.

Typically, people come into therapy groups, as they come into any group setting, individuated. Given that in our culture people are socialized to an individuated learning and development model, this is completely understandable. They say things like, "I had this awful fight with my mother last night. I was furious . . . and I'm really upset right now"; "I feel really crazy, like I'm not here, and it scares me." They look to the therapist for some advice, solution, interpretation, explanation (or, in what are referred to as post-modern therapies, leadership in a collaborative process that might generate some new understanding of themselves).[8] They want to feel better and have more control over their lives.

People come to social therapy with similar understandings and expectations, even if they have heard that, unlike most therapies which are geared to problem solving and reducing symptoms, it is a developmental approach. They may have even been told in their initial therapy session that social therapy is designed to help people exercise their collective power to create new emotional growth. To most new clients this sounds appealing, if ineffable. And so most clients become group members. Once in group, they find their individuated mode of relating to their emotionality practically-critically challenged through the work/play/struggle to create a new socialized helping environment.

The members of social therapy groups come together each week and participate in creating their group. In this process, they learn and develop new emotionality. The social therapist works with the group (rather than with the individuated selves that comprise the group) to organize itself as an *emotional zpd*. The various members, each at different levels of emotional development, are encouraged (invited, supported, challenged) to create *the group's* level of emotional development. This ongoing and ever-changing activity, it turns out, is developmental for all – including those who are most "individually" developed.

Members of the group raise whatever they want and however they want (typically, how they're feeling, an emotional problem, a relationship going bad, something upsetting that happened to them, and the like). The work of the group is figuring out how to talk about what they want to talk about. Why is this the group's task? Because the language of emotionality – consisting of a relatively small group of "inner-located objects," such as anger, panic, depression, shame, jealousy, anxiety, and so on – is pain producing. There is perhaps nothing, in Western cultures at least, that people relate to in language and thought as more fundamentally individuated and less social than feelings. Feelings are the bottom line: "These are MY feelings. That's how I feel." Beginning and end of story. What this understanding and way of speaking does is leave people isolated and alone with "possession" of their feelings. Once entrapped in that way there is no basis on which to get better, to escape from the trap. Creating the social therapy group is creating a relational understanding and language of emotionality, and this collective activity can be a way out of the trap.

"How can we talk so that our talking helps build the group?" This challenge is the focus of the group building process. The group's task is to babble, play with language, creatively imitate and complete each other and the therapist, and make meaning together. Speaking as truth telling, reality representing, inner thought and feeling revealing, these deeply held beliefs of the functions of language are challenged as people falteringly attempt to converse in new ways, to create something new out of their initial individuated, problem-oriented presentations of self.

The social therapist's task is to lead the group in this activity of discovering a method of relating to emotional talk relationally rather than individualistically and as activistic rather than as representational. In this process people come to appreciate what – and that – they can create, and simultaneously to realize the limitations of trying to learn, grow and create individually. If and as the group gradually comes to understand this, members (at different moments) realize that *growth comes from participating in the process of building the groups in which one functions*. This new learning, in a Vygotskian, zpd-like fashion, rekindles development – development by virtue of the group growing. Traditional therapy's focus – the individuated self who discovers deeper insights into his or her consciousness – is transformed in social therapy into the collective engaged in the continuous activity of creating a new social unit, the emotional zpd. The therapeutic question transforms as well, from

"How is each individual doing?" to "How well is the group performing its activity?"

This shift in focus from the individual to the group is not a denial of the individual, but rather a reshaping and reorganization of what is traditionally related to as a dualistic and antagonistic relationship into a dialectical one. On the one hand, mainstream psychology has tended to negate the group or reduce the group to the individual. On the other hand, mainstream Marxism has tended to negate the individual or reduce the individual to the group. But one does not have to be negated or reduced to the other, and in recognizing the groupness of human life, social therapy does not negate individuals. The group is engaged in producing something collectively. As is the case with many life activities, individual members contribute to different degrees and in different ways to the process-and-product.

The therapeutic zpd-creating activity is a relearning of how to learn developmentally, by which I mean collectively and noncognitively overdetermined. As I have discussed, Vygotsky showed that children learn collectively and through their active relationships with others at varying levels of skill, knowledge, expertise, ability and personality. They are not yet socialized to the cultural norm that one *must know*. They have not yet evolved the epistemic posture. They learn by doing with others what they do not know how to do because the group (usually the family) supports such active, creative risk taking and performs with them. Most people have not done this since they were very young, and so they have to relearn how to do it in ways appropriate to being adults. Social therapy is one such way, sharing important similarities with the active, ensemble, performatory, noncognitive and nondidactic zpd of early childhood.

COMPLETION

I characterized social therapy, above, as a method of relating to emotional talk relationally and activistically. Here, I will "unpack" both what I mean by that and its relation to reading Vygotsky social therapeutically. To do so, I take us back to Newman's puzzle: What is going on in therapy that makes talking about one's inner life helpful when there is no such thing as an inner life? Eventually, Newman and I discovered the solution in Vygotsky's writings on thinking and speaking and the sociality of language (primarily from *Thinking and Speech*).

Vygotsky's accounting of how children develop as speakers of a language seemed a reasonable fit with what was going on in social therapy in the sense that the adult clients are being supported by the therapists to do what is beyond them – to create new ways of speaking and listening to each other, and new ways to understand and relate to talk and to emotionality. By their language play, they are creating new performances of themselves as a way out of the rigidified roles, patterns and identities that cause so much emotional pain. What must language – in particular, the speaking of it – be in order for this to be the case?

For years Newman and I talked about this, sharing views of language and revisiting some of the philosophical, psychological and linguistics thinkers that had influenced us, for ideas and insight. In this process, Newman reviewed and I read for the first time the later writings of Wittgenstein (for example, *Philosophical Investigations*, 1953, and *The Blue and Brown Books*, 1965). In doing so we realized how strongly Wittgenstein had influenced Newman's therapeutic work and how therapeutic Wittgenstein's philosophy was (something noted by a few Wittgenstein scholars, for example, Baker, 1992).

Seen therapeutically, Wittgenstein was attempting to cure philosophers of their illness, manifest in the intellectual and emotional muddles they get into by the way they think about thought and language. What they do is locate thought "inside," with language as the outward expression or representation of it, and then search for causes, correspondences, rules and parallels between the two. What if, Wittgenstein asks, there are none? What if the particular way language has come to be used and understood creates pictures that hold us captive (Wittgenstein, 1953), and *that's* what makes the muddle?[9] Wittgenstein developed a method to help free philosophers from such traps. In a myriad of ways and hundreds of examples, he showed that the *expressionist* picture of communication – that people have an inner life that gets expressed in language – was defective. To him, language was better understood as the activity of speaking, as a form of life ("The term 'language-game' is meant to bring into prominence the fact that the *speaking* of language is part of an activity, or of a form of life," Wittgenstein, 1953, para. 23).[10]

This analysis was helpful in shedding some light on the process of social therapy. Making the analogy with Wittgenstein, social therapy is a method to help ordinary people get free from some of the constraints of language and from "versions of philosophical pathologies that permeate everyday life" (Newman and Holzman, 1996/2006, p. 171). Having the task of the social therapy group be to create the group exposes ways of talking that perpetuate experiencing ourselves as individuated products, at the same time as it generates new ways of talking. Wittgenstein's conception of language games as a form of life helped us see that social therapy groups are makers of meaning, and not simply users of language.

However, something was still missing. If the expressionist conception of language was inaccurate, then what *is* going on when people are speaking? If our thoughts, ideas, feelings, beliefs and so on, are not somehow "transported" from our minds to other people through language and other means of communication, what is happening when we speak with each other? If language is not a mediator between an inner life and outer reality, then what is it? How is it possible for people to make meaning together?

Back to Vygotsky. In his extensive discussion of the relationship between thinking and speaking, Vygotsky provided some innovative answers to these questions. Like Wittgenstein, he challenged the expressionist view of language. Speaking, he said, is not the outward expression of thinking, but part of a unified, transformative process. Two passages from *Thinking and Speech* are especially clear in characterizing his alternative understanding:

> The relationship of thought to word is not a thing but a process, a movement from thought to word and from word to thought. . . . Thought is not expressed but completed in the word. We can, therefore, speak of the establishment (i.e., the unity of being and nonbeing) of thought in the word. Any thought strives to unify, to establish a relationship between one thing and another. Any thought has movement. It unfolds.
>
> (Vygotsky, 1987, p. 250)

> The structure of speech is not simply the mirror image of the structure of thought. It cannot, therefore, be placed on thought like clothes off a rack. Speech does not merely serve as the expression of developed thought. Thought is restructured as it is transformed into speech. It is not expressed but completed in the word.
>
> (Vygotsky, 1987, p. 251)

If, as Vygotsky appears to be saying, language and thought are a dialectical process, a unified activity, then the dualistic divide between inner and outer vanishes. There are no longer two separate worlds, the private one of thinking and the social one of speaking. There is, instead, the complex dialectical unity, speaking/thinking, in which speaking *completes* thinking.

This alternative to the expressionist view of language is an elegant fit with Vygotsky's articulation of the sociality of language development in children. The child would not be able to perform as a speaker (and thereby learn to speak) if thinking/speaking were not a continuously *socially completive activity* (Newman and Holzman, 1993). For, if speaking is the completing of thinking, if the process is continuously creative in socio-cultural space (that is, if mind is in society), then it follows that the "completer" does not have to be the one who is doing the thinking. Others can complete for us. In doing so, they are no more saying *what* we are thinking than *we* are saying what we are thinking when we complete ourselves. Remember: Thought is not expressed in the word! In the conversations (language games) that babbling babies and their speaking caregivers create, socially completive activity is ongoing, with both baby and others doing the completing. Beyond baby-hood, this suggests that when people are speaking, what they are doing is *not saying* what's going on but *creating* what's going on, and that what is called "understanding each other" comes about by virtue of engaging in this activity. In therapy, talking about one's inner life is therapeutic because and to the extent that it is a socially completive activity and not a transmittal of private states of mind. The human ability to create with language – to complete, and be completed by, others – is, for adults as well as for very young children, a continuous process of creating who we are becoming, a tool-and-result of the activity of developing.

I doubt that Vygotsky would be completely comfortable with the way that social therapy plays with his conception of thought being completed in the word. Understanding language as a socially completive activity raises questions about "the truth" of people's words and, by extension, the concept of truth itself. On his part, Vygotsky was a believer in truth; his rejection of universals and objective–subjective dualism did not extend that far. For him, truth was to be discovered in the creating of a Marxist psychology.

In our times, however, truth is being called into question by philosophers, social scientists and even scientists. Among these are psychologists and psychotherapists who reject an expressionist view of language and with it the notion of *objective* truth. For them, talk therapy is not done in order to discover some hidden truth of someone's life, to find the true cause of emotional pain or to apply the one true method of treatment, because truth in that form (Truth) does not exist. Instead, they construct subjective theories of truth and devise practices consistent with them. Here we can point to social constructionists, who search for relational forms of dialogue as an alternative to objectivist-based debate and criticism (McNamee and Gergen, 1992, 1999); narrative therapists, who work to expose the "storiness" of our lives and help people create their own (and, most often, better) stories (McLeod, 1997; Monk *et al.*, 1997; Rosen and Kuehlwein, 1996; White, 2007; White and Epston, 1990); and collaborative therapists, who emphasize the dynamic and co-constructed nature of meaning (e.g. Anderson, 1997; Anderson and Gehart, 2007; Paré and Larner, 2004; Strong and Paré, 2004).

In proposing that truth is subjective and that there can exist multiple truths (all with a small "t"), these approaches do not escape objective–subjective dualism but rather merely flip it over. Truth may be socially constructed in these approaches, but dualism remains intact, as there must be something *about which* it can be said, "It is true (or false)." In contrast, relating to therapeutic talk as performance, and to clients as an ensemble of performers who, along with the therapist, are staging a new therapeutic conversation each session is meant as a rejection of truth (and its opposite, falsity) in favor of *socially completive activity*. The social therapeutic shift to activity is a way to transform therapeutic talk from being an appeal to or about objective, outer reality Truth or subjective, inner cognitive or emotive truths. As socially completive activity, therapy talk is a consciously self-reflexive engagement of the creating of the talk itself. In performing therapy the fictional nature of "the truth" of our everyday language, our everyday psychology and our everyday stories gets exposed as people have the opportunity to experience themselves as the collective creators of their emotional activity (Newman, 1999).

A woman began a social therapy group saying that she still hated her father. She couldn't be absolutely sure, but she thought he was always out to abuse her; he looked at her in a certain way, etc. The initial response of several group members – a line of questioning that is typical in this kind of situation – was to ask for details (what happened, when, for how long, etc.) in order to find out what "really" happened, was she "really" abused, etc. – that is, in order to get to the "truth." After about 20 minutes, the focus of the conversation shifted, as the group began to inquire about what this woman meant by some of the words she was saying ("What do you mean when you say 'you hate him'?"; "What do you mean by 'abuse'?") and how it was that she was saying them ("Why are you saying this to us now?"). The group began to "do meaning" as they explored particular words and phrases in the specific contextualization of their talk. They stopped doing talk as truth telling in favor of exploring the activity of their speaking together. This changed activity – from trying to find the truth to creating meanings – typically creates a group sense of new meaning, rather than a collective sense of truth. Engaging in this activity, the group can gain a heightened understanding that finding truth is not possible, that meanings are created collectively and that they have the power to create meanings. In the words of one group member:

> The challenge in our group is always to not take what's said as truth. We don't always succeed! It's very freeing, though, when I can hear and see what so-and-so is saying and doing and not experience it as "This is really what they're doing and so this is what I have to do in response." People say words and we don't know what they mean until we create their meaning. The group grows a lot by taking ownership of what it creates.
>
> (Holzman and Newman, with Strong, 2004, pp. 82–83)

I would be remiss, especially with regard to readers familiar with Vygotsky but not with psychotherapy, if I did not mention how more cognitively oriented Vygotskians think about therapy and the therapeutic process. In doing so, I may be helping you to get a better glimpse of the therapeutic Vygotsky that I see. (It is worth noting, however, that the number of articles and papers on Vygotsky and psychotherapy can, even today, be counted on one hand.)

A recent article by Portes (2005, under review) suggests ways that cultural-historical activity theory could and should be applied to counseling and psychotherapy. Portes provides an historical, cultural and meta-psychological analysis of why this approach has received so little attention from mainstream mental health disciplines. He then presents the approach and aspects of it, particularly Vygotsky's work, that he sees as relevant to the practice of counseling and psychotherapy. His version of activity theory is the conventional, cognitively overdetermined one of motivated actions and mediational tools discussed in Chapter 1 (this volume, pp. 15–17), and his vision of therapy is the conventional one of solving individuated problems (abnormalities in higher psychological functioning). Both can be seen in the following excerpt:

> In the psychotherapy process, the acquisition or internalization of skills, beliefs and attitudes on the part of the client is often the goal of the treatment or activity. The advice, insight, suggestions or skills offered by the therapist directly or incidentally represent a menu of neutral stimuli any one of which the client might appropriate and employ to change the future. Therapy, like education, offers a construction zone for meanings and skills to be developed.
>
> (Portes, 2005, under review, p. 28)

To Portes, helping people therapeutically is essentially an educational enterprise that can be advanced with the concept of the zpd, in that it can help the therapist focus on the client's learning potential and design learning activities that are "in" the zpd. The word "emotion" never appears in the article.

Tharp takes the analogy of psychotherapy with education even further in his article entitled, "Therapist as teacher: A developmental model of psychotherapy" (1999). He proposes a model that transfers to therapy many of the tenets derived from a sociocultural approach to pedagogical research, especially the concept of the zpd as instrumental scaffold. Like Portes, Tharp's cognitively overdetermined vision of psychotherapy is clear. He writes that the fundamental task of therapy is "the development of more effective higher-order processes involving analysis application, modification, and mastery of those processes, and the eventual incorporation of them into the overall schemas by which they understand their lives" (Tharp, 1999, p. 23).[11]

Both Tharp and Portes are inspired by Vygotsky to propose that psychotherapy could be advanced if we apply a cognitive rendering of Vygotsky's developmental psychology to it and begin to see the therapist as teacher. Anticipating my discussions of education and learning in school and outside of school settings in Chapters 3 and 4, my proposal goes in the opposite direction, namely, that education could be advanced if we consider the teacher as therapist.

Chapter 3

In the classroom

Learning to perform and performing to learn

> The problem is not that we've set the bar too high and failed but that we've set the bar too low and succeeded.
>
> (Sir Ken Robinson, "Do schools kill creativity?")

"Teacher as therapist" – my counter suggestion to "Therapist as teacher" (Tharp, 1999) – was only half serious. The cognitive–emotive divide is what makes it so. While I do think that schools would be friendlier places than they are now if they merely flipped the coin and gave students (of any age) the chance to speak about and get help with how they are feeling, that is not what I am suggesting. To me, teacher as therapist means organizing the learning environment performatorily, because it is performance that keeps us away from the paradigmatic dualism of cognition and emotion. Teacher as therapist means helping students develop as learners, which involves the entirety of a person's makeup and not just his or her "cognitive faculties."

In the beginning of this book I pointed to the negative view there is of emotions, including their secondary status relative to cognition in psychology and the broader culture. I also noted how the culture (including institutionalized psychology) has shaped people to see their lives and the world in general in terms of problems and how the problem-solution paradigm has been misapplied to human subjectivity. More than any other social organization I can think of, education has brought the negative view of emotions and the problem paradigm together with a vengeance. Mainstream psychotherapy may insist that a person has an emotional problem in order to get help, but it doesn't view emotionality per se as problematic. Not so schools. Structurally (by which I mean how they are organized) schools relate to emotions as problems, even the "positive" emotions. (How often do classroom teachers *not* stop infectious laughter and silliness? Or linger with a student's momentary happiness? Or share their own excitement about something?) Not all play is emotionally pleasant, but the nearly total taboo on play in American schools (at this time, even in kindergartens) must have something to do with its frequently transparent enjoyment. As for anger, upsetness, frustration and other "negative" emotional displays, these are considered serious problems in schools, understood to interfere with learning and, increasingly, to be symptomatic of an individual's neurological abnormality or psychopathology. Fortunately, many, many teachers are able to organize their classrooms and student relationships in ways that recognize and are respectful of emotions, despite official educational policy and ideology to the contrary.

Such misunderstanding and devaluing of emotionality is, of course, not new or confined to the USA or to other wealthy, industrialized countries. What is new is that today it has the imprimatur of science and medicine. Three quarters of a century ago, when Vygotsky critiqued the cognitive–emotive divide and generated a socio-cultural theory of developmental learning in its place, both psychology and mass public education were in their infancy (the latter was nonexistent in tsarist Russia, and Vygotsky was working to establish it in the new Soviet Union). Had his views not fallen out of favor under Stalinist rule (and perhaps had he not died so young, in 1934), they might have been put into practice.

Vygotsky insisted that a human psychology not be concerned with particulars but rather with unities – the unity of the person; the unity of the person and its social relations; and the unity of person, social relations and culture. When he discussed higher psychological processes he was not referring to cognition separate from emotion. On the contrary, he believed that the separation of intellect and affect was "one of the most basic defects of traditional approaches to the study of psychology," and that those who do so are left with thinking as "divorced from the full vitality of life, from the motives, interests, and inclinations of the thinking individual" (Vygotsky, 1987, p. 50). Rather than isolating one from the other, Vygotsky proposed that "there exists a dynamic meaningful system that constitutes *a unity of affective and intellectual processes*" (Vygotsky, 1987, p. 50, original emphasis). However, the great majority of psychologists of learning and educational researchers influenced by Vygotsky have made that separation, essentially erasing affect from the higher psychological processes picture and perpetuating "a one-sided view of the human personality" (Vygotsky, 1983, Vol. 3, p. 57, quoted in Gajdamaschko, 2005, p. 14).[1]

Over the past decade articles have begun to appear in the literature that look seriously at this unintentional bias and introduce correctives that will give emotions their due in the teaching and learning process. For example, Lisa Goldstein, in an article entitled, "The relational zone: The role of caring relationships in the co-construction of mind" (1999), is concerned that current educational applications of Vygotsky's zpd are oversimplified by excluding the affective, noting that this is understandable in light of the fact that there is little elaboration of this topic in Vygotsky's writings. Goldstein's corrective is to broaden the zpd to include not only the interpersonal dimension but also the "interrelational dimension [which] is a shared affective space created by the adult and the child in the ZPD" (Goldstein, 1999, p. 651). She draws upon the notion of the ethic of care from feminist moral theory, particularly as developed by Nel Noddings (1984), to generate a language to talk about the interrelational dimension of the zpd. [See also Nelmes (2000) and DiPardo and Schnack (2004) for examples of empirical research that incorporate an emotional dimension to the zpd in examining the teaching-learning process.]

Recognizing that learning is emotional and reconceptualizing the zpd to incorporate the affective dimension is a welcome reform of the dominant educational model, but far more is needed. As I see it, all the educational reforms taken together (Vygotskian-based and otherwise) could not transform schools into developmental learning environments. By developmental learning environments I mean those that are organized for everyone involved to participate in the collective, tool-and-result activity of creating "learning-leading-development." As I discussed in Chapter 2 in relation to psychotherapy, this entails relating to people as capable of doing what they do not know how to do, namely, creating the very environments that create their growth. When this happens people discover not only how to do what they do not know how to do, but equally important, *that* they can do it.

The discovery *that* they can do some activity (let us shorten it to "that-ness") is, I believe, a component of learning for very young children that is usually lost once they enter school. In the first few years the child's life is not separated into times for "living in the world" and "learning about things in the world," and so learning is part of doing what the child and others do together. Because it is fused with the everyday relational life of human beings (the creating of culture), that which is learned (saying "more" while reaching out one's hand, for example) is, at the same time, a learning that this is something that people do (in other words, the that-ness of speaking to each other, of saying words while doing some action). This kind of self-reflexivity is no more conscious for the very young child than "learning how to learn" [taken to be an aspect of learning at least since Bateson (1972)]; indeed, "learning that" may well be what accounts for "learning how" (Holzman and Newman, 1987; Hood, Fiess and Aron, 1982; Newman and Holzman, 1993). Furthermore, it may well account for how it is that learning in the first few years of life is so rapidly and qualitatively transformative. In their improvisational, creative and playful engagement with caretakers, siblings, peers, pets, toys and other objects, and media, there is no separation between learner, teacher and what is learned. Each instance of learning something is simultaneously an instance of developing as a learner.

In great contrast, schools function with an acquisitional learning model rather than a developmental one (Holzman, 1997a). The acquisitional model associates learning with knowing, and organizes teaching and learning around the production, dissemination and construction of knowledge. The task of the typical school is the production of knowers, not learners (see, for example, Rothstein, 1994). Public education has always been this way; it – and its failure – is more obvious now because current educational policy is *officially* acquisitionally oriented (No Child Left Behind Act of 2001/Public Law 107-110). The socio-cultural, developmental aspects of learning (or, learning-leading-development) – learning how to learn, learning that one is a learner, learning that learning is something human beings do (as well as learning that reading, writing, math, science, etc. are things that people do) – are all but lost.

If what I have said is even partially accurate, then the people in schools need a lot of help! If schools are not developmental, what is to be done? My long-term answer is to dismantle schools. [I am not alone in favoring this; for example Bard College (New York) president Leon Botstein has been outspoken in his view that high schools should be abolished, see Epstein (2007).] My short-term answer is threefold: (a) create ways to bring (even a little) development into schools; (b) simultaneously create spaces for developmental learning to flourish outside of schools; and (c) bring both of these to bear on the continuous re-education of the public, the politicians and the policy makers.[2] Some of the work being done outside of schools will be discussed in Chapter 4.

DEVELOPMENTAL LEARNING AND PLAY

It is more than a little ironic that children play school but are not allowed to play *in* school. It is tragically misguided and myopic. The fact that children can play school, both before they ever go to one and once they are in school, is remarkable and remarkably important. I would go so far as to say that it holds the "secret" to eliminating learning failure. But educators and educational researchers have, apparently, not been able to see it that way.

Kindergarten classes have less play and more academics, primary schools eliminate recess period, and both primary and secondary schools cut out physical education.[3] With these and other changes like them, one could almost say that the official position on play is that it is irrelevant to school learning. Among scholars, the study of play does not have an official home in the American Educational Research Association (AERA), the 25,000-member organization of educators, psychologists and other social scientists concerned with improving education by encouraging scholarly inquiry related to education and evaluation. AERA is organized into 12 broad areas of interest (including administration; learning and instruction; measurement and research methodology; teaching and learning). To meet the "special interests" of its diverse membership, it allows members to petition for the establishment of a SIG (Special Interest Group), and thereby gain legitimacy and the right to organize a membership and present scholarly work at AERA meetings. There are over 160 SIGS. Play is not among them, and the 2006 petition to establish a play SIG was denied. (Official psychology is even less interested in play. As far as I can tell, there has never been a move to petition for a play division in the 100,000+ member APA and the topic is not a presence in its divisions of educational or school psychology.)

Fortunately, things happen in spite of and outside of officialdom. Play – in early childhood and throughout the life span, and in relation to learning and development – is receiving growing attention. The ideas and practical work I am presenting here are necessarily limited but interested readers are referred to Blatner (1997), Göncü and Gaskins (2007), Kane (1995), Nachmanovitch (1990), Reifel (1999), Sawyer (1997, 2007), Sutton-Smith (2001), Terr (1999), as well as the books and articles mentioned in Chapter 5 that discuss play in organizations.

In Chapter 2 (this volume, pp. 31–32) I touched briefly on what Vygotsky had to say about play. It is time to take a closer look.

When people speak of play in everyday talk or academic discourse it usually has one or another of these meanings: *free play*, such as the pretend and fantasy activities of early childhood; *game play*, the more structured and explicitly rule-governed activities that become common in the school years and then dominant in adulthood; or *theatrical play or performance*, common in early childhood and, in adulthood, primarily in formalized and professional versions. My reading of Vygotsky has helped me see the importance of all three types of play for lifelong developmental learning.

About the first kind of play, the free play of early childhood, Vygotsky wrote, "a child's greatest achievements are possible in play" (1987, p. 100). For him, the unique feature of free play is the creation of an imaginary situation in which meaning dominates action. He identified two defining characteristics of play – an imaginary situation and rules – and described how the relationship between the two changes as different kinds of play develop. All play, he said, creates an imaginary situation and all imaginary situations contain rules. In the play of very young children the imaginary situation – playing Mommy and baby, for example – dominates, and the rules come into existence at the same time and through the creation of the imaginary situation, that is, in the playing. They are "not rules that are formulated in advance and that change during the course of the game but ones that stem from an imaginary situation" (1978, p. 95).

In game play, the rules are overt, and the more complex the game the more the rules dominate over the imaginary situation. To illustrate, Vygotsky suggests that even a simple game in which candy represents something inedible contains the rule, don't eat the candy. In a game of chess, however, the overt rules clearly dominate over the imaginary situation of the contest among knights, queens, etc. (Vygotsky, 1978, p. 95). Using contemporary examples, playing basketball, football, video games and board games requires knowing the pre-established rules.

This interplay of imagination – which frees – and rules – which constrain – is key to the developmental potential of play, Vygotsky told us. The action created in the "imaginative sphere" frees the players from situational constraints and, at the same time, imposes constraints of its own. In this way, "play creates a zone of proximal development of the child. In play a child always behaves beyond his average age, above his daily behavior; in play it is as though he were a head taller than himself" (1978, p. 102).

The zpd of play has unique characteristics, Vygotsky pointed out:

> Though the play–development relationship can be compared to the instruction–development relationship, play provides a much wider background for changes in needs and conscious-ness. Action in the imaginative sphere, in an imaginary situation, the creation of voluntary intentions, and the forma-tion of real-life plans and volitional motives – all appear in play and make it the highest level of preschool development.
>
> (1978, pp. 102–103)

This analysis of play is fascinating. You can go places with it. Methodologically, for example, it inspired Newman and me to think about rules and tools. The rules of the free play of early childhood, those that come into existence simultaneous with playing, we understand as "rule-and-result" – analogous to tool-and-result. The rules of later game play, those that are set up beforehand, we understand as "rule for result" – analogous to tool for result (Newman and Holzman, 1993, pp. 100–101). *Play is a leading factor in development, then, because it is a rule-and-result activity, not a rule for result one.* Playing without rules/without knowing how/without knowing the rules is pretty much the daily activity of preschool children. I have already pointed out the importance of adults and older children playing language games with infants and toddlers well before they know how to speak and many years before they know the rules of grammar (or even that that there are rules of grammar). They play many, many kinds of "games without rules" with them – dressing games, eating games, going bye-bye games, reading games, watching TV games, going to sleep games, taking a bath games, and so on. And in their free play young children make up rules in the course of creating their imaginary situation ("You're the Mommy and you feed the baby like this, OK?").

The kind of freedom from environmental constraints ("reality") that Vygotsky identified in free (rule-and-result) play has similarities with another kind of play – theatrical play, or performance, especially the unscripted, improvisational kind. In both free and theatrical play, the players are more directly the producers of their activity, in charge of generating and coordinating the perceptual, cognitive and emotional elements of the play. When I look at children's free play with this performance lens, I see the value of play in a new light.

For most psychologists and educators the value of play is that it facilitates the learning of social-cultural roles. In conventional activity-theoretic terms, play is an instrumental tool that serves to mediate between the individual and the culture (as in the work of Nicolopoulou and Cole, 1993; Rogoff, 1990; Rogoff and Lave, 1984; Wertsch, 1985). Through acting out roles (play acting), children "try out" the roles they will soon take on in "real life." While I agree that play can be done and understood that way, I think doing so skips over the paradox of free, pretend play – when children are pretending, they are least like what they are pretending to be. When they play school they are *least* like teachers and students because teachers and students in school are not playing at being teachers and students, but rather acting out their societally determined roles. Children playing school, or Mommy and Daddy, or Harry Potter and Dumbledore, are not acting out predetermined roles. They are creating new performances of themselves – at once the playwrights, directors and performers. They are creating culture. This is how I make sense of Vygotsky's understanding that in play the child acts as though a head taller (Vygotsky, 1978, p.102) – that the developmental potential of play is as *performed activity* and not as behavioral acting.

In the process of adapting to rule for result play and rule-governed behavior, the occasions for rule-and-result play (performed activity) lessen. This kind of "pointless" play becomes less valued and less appropriate once children enter school. Once having learned to play by the rules, it is difficult to continue playing without rules. That this is how things currently are organized need not imply that Vygotsky's analysis, or the implications I draw from reframing it in performance language, remain within the confines of early child development. Play might indeed be the highest level of preschool development ("a leading activity," Vygotsky called it, 1978, p. 103), but it would be a mistake to infer from this that play's developmental potential is limited to the preschool years.[4]

Ironically, Vygotsky himself appears to have made this mistake. He discovered what children's play is and why it is critical to development in early childhood, but his writings strongly suggest that he believed it did not serve this purpose in later years, but lost its significance to formalized learning (1978, pp. 102–103). I think that he discovered that "secret" to eliminating learning failure I mentioned above, but failed to see the kind of discovery it was, namely, the discovery that in order for learning past early childhood to be developmental, it needs to be done playfully.

My Institute colleagues and I have tried to bring playful learning into schools in a number of ways, from creating our own school to training public school teachers. As you read my descriptions of these projects and their successes and failures, keep in mind that the goal has not been to reform schools but rather to help the people in them learn developmentally – to the extent that this is realizable in environments not set up for them to do so. The method we have come to is to create with children and adults ways to play/perform school and bring play/performance into schools.

PLAYING SCHOOL

For 12 years, from 1985–1997, the Institute was involved in designing and running an experimental school in New York City where the Vygotsky I discovered through social therapy could be played with for educational rather than psychotherapeutic purposes. It was a wonderfully wild and crazy place. The school was small (with 20–40 students at any one time). Initially, most of the students were from Harlem poor and working-class African American families, but over the years Afro-Caribbean and white students from different areas of the city also enrolled, in most cases because they were having trouble in traditional public schools. While the school was by no means for everyone, for those who stayed with it, and the many who volunteered, studied and visited from many parts of the world, it was a very special "school for growth" (Holzman, 1997a). It was, as well, a coming together of the African American community schools movement and the Marx- and Vygotsky-influenced activity-theoretic methodology of the Institute and its broader community.

When I first met Barbara Taylor she was principal of the St Thomas Community School in Harlem, a primary school she had founded. At 62 years old, Taylor had already enjoyed a long career as an educator – she had been an elementary school teacher, reading specialist, assistant principal, principal, and founder of a community school. Courageous and energetic, Taylor had been guided by her commitment to helping poor children learn and grow. As principal of the St Thomas School, which operated under the auspices of the archdiocese of New York, she led a group of parents in a prolonged fight against the Church bureaucracy when, after Taylor had successfully raised supplementary funds for enriching the school's programming, the officials decided to withdraw its usual funding – conveying to Taylor and the families that these children did not need or deserve enrichment. The result was the formation of the independent St Thomas Community School, with Taylor as principal.

After several years, Taylor felt that St Thomas's organization as a dynamic community school had gone as far as it could. She felt she needed a new methodology with which to build a school environment where children would be more challenged and supported to be successful learners, the kind of learners they are in the preschool years. Taylor came to the Institute, shared her story, asked us to help her transform her practice, and our collaboration began. Taylor resigned from the St Thomas Community School and, taking several families with her, became principal of the new Barbara Taylor School for grades K through 8.

During its first 6 years, the Barbara Taylor School concentrated on creating conditions for children to be emotionally supported and challenged in order to be able to learn. Taylor was always prepared not only with smiles and hugs, but also food and extra articles of clothing, for children who came to school hungry or without socks, hats or gloves. Wonderful and necessary, said Newman and I, but not enough. We felt that everyone at the school, including the teachers and administrators, needed to do some work to develop emotionally if the children were to have a chance at becoming good learners. We began a campaign designed to "Stop Abusive Behavior." The abuse at issue was not physical, but relational, and so routine as to pass unnoticed, despite the emotional toll it instills: the way adults humiliate students and students humiliate one another; the standard practice of teaching to tests with no regard for the learning process; the insistence on following rules that have only to do with adults asserting their authority; and the classism, racism, sexism and homophobia that are ingrained in schools and teaching practices. Taylor launched this project by asking the students to share how she was abusive to them; one way, they told her, was "that" look she gave them. From there, discussions moved to how students were abusive to her, to other staff and to one another. Students and teachers created a variety of improvisational activities and, eventually, policies out of these conversations as responses to the question, "What can/should we do about abuse?" This project was the foundation for what became a continuous and continuously transforming process of collectively creating an emotionally supportive – by which I mean therapeutic, by which I mean developmental – learning environment.

During these years, the school's motto was "developing children as leaders" (Strickland and Holzman, 1989), meaning people who take risks to take responsibility. The school modified a standard curriculum to support student participation and encourage activism. Much of the classroom work was interdisciplinary; peer teaching and tutoring of younger students by older students were regular features of the school day; and the student body as a whole was frequently in courtrooms or marching in demonstrations for human and civil rights. Barbara Taylor School students' achievement scores on standardized tests exceeded those of public school students in the district – and they learned without being coerced or abused. [See LaCerva (1992) and Strickland and Holzman (1989), for discussions of this phase in the life of the Barbara Taylor School.]

To Newman's and my taste, however, the school was too much like school – too focused on learning "about" and not enough on "learning that." We were eager to develop the approach further in a Vygotskian direction which, to us, meant to create the school as a continuously emerging environment where learning leads development. How could the zpds of early childhood – in and by which children freely and enthusiastically do what they do not know how to do – be recreated in ways appropriate for school-aged children? Unlike babies and toddlers, older children not only know a lot of things; they also know that knowing is valued, that there are things one is supposed to know by a certain age, and that not knowing them has consequences. Regardless of whether they are good or bad knowers, they have taken on the epistemic posture. At the same time, older children have increased their repertoire of play and, in addition to pretend play, they have learned and enjoy rule for result, game play and, in certain forms, theatrical play. The challenge was to put to use these three types of play to create a performatory environment in and by which they could consciously take on a new "performance posture."

The vision we had was of groupings of people of different ages creating a constant flow of interrelated and overlapping zpds. We removed what we took to be obstacles to this process, including grade levels and curricula, in order to increase opportunities for spontaneous, unsystematic and heterogeneous groupings to come together and drift apart and play without rules, to create perform-ances as readers, writers, scientists, historians, test makers, artists, mathematicians, poets, and so on. To let students, their parents and the community know the extent to which the heart of the Barbara Taylor School was "learning is social," the school reopened after the summer in 1991 with the declaration that "We teach your child to CHEAT," which stood for Children Helping to Educate Another Training (see Holzman, 1993 for a description of this transition).

Housed in a Harlem brownstone and then a Brooklyn store-front, from 1991–1997 the Barbara Taylor School was a combi-nation one-room schoolhouse, three-ring circus, international visitor and volunteer center, and home base for students and staff. There was a steady stream of college interns, guest teachers and parents, and hardly a week went by without a visit from a psychologist, educator, university student or entire class from another school somewhere in the world. Our most honored guest was Lev Vygotsky's daughter, Gita L'vovna Vygodskaya, who is herself a psychologist. Each day school began with the same task: How shall we perform school today? Visitors and itinerant participants were invited to join whatever happened to be going on – constructing "standardized" tests, playing Jeopardy or Uno, creating a game show to help a child learn to spell, constructing a model city, doing historical research – and to give freely of their curiosity, expertise and ideas for what might happen next (Holzman, 1997a).

In social therapeutic language, the task of the group (the school) was to perform school. In Vygotsky's language, it was to create method as simultaneously tool and result. In a synthesis of the two, it was to create the stage and the performance simultaneously by playing in such a way (the way very young children do) that rules are not formulated in advance but stem from the imaginary situation of the play and emerge in the playing. Each day, the students and adults would decide together what they were going to do, what kind of learning performances they were going to create. The teachers (referred to as learning directors) were not there to facilitate learning but rather to direct themselves and the students in this kind of play and to keep the performatory in ongoing activities.[5]

When one or more students did not want to perform or disrupted an ongoing performance by others, keeping the activity performatory was most challenging – given the strong tendency to step out of the scene and reprimand or remove the disruption. This situation came up again and again, providing opportunities for making alternative responses that incorporated the refusal to perform or the disruption into the performance. Among the responses I recall are the following. Someone saying, "OK, let's include in this scene 'the pain in the butt' who keeps bothering us." Or, "Let's all play the interrupting game" (and then everyone talks at once). Or (directed to the person who is interrupting), "If you really can't wait to say what you have to say, then say it again, but this time say it louder and with more emotion." At other times, the performance might be stopped and taken as an opportunity for the group to grapple with what they wanted to do with the changed situation.

The life of babies and toddlers is a nearly endless stream of activities in which they stop what they are doing and create something new out of it, either by doing it again (and perhaps again and again) or by doing something entirely different. Children in schools rarely have this critically important life experience; they are supposed to do exactly what they are told, stay on task until it is completed, and not make mistakes. Consciously created performance allows school-aged children and adults to "do the scene over again." Giving them this opportunity has been my motivation for devising ways for them to learn–feel–relate–live performatorily.

Among the many things it was to me, the Barbara Taylor School was a place I could nourish my long-standing interest in language development. The years of producing its performance as a school broadened my understanding of who becomes – and what it means to become – a speaker of a language. It was during this same time that I had realized the import of Vygotsky's description of the language-learning zpd and how very young children learn to talk and use language by babbling and engaging in the activity of meaning making. It was also when Newman and I transformed Vygotsky's discoveries into a way to see that adults in social therapy groups were creating new ways of speaking and listening (another kind of babble) and new ways of relating to talk and emotionality. If this was what babies and their caretakers and social therapy groups were doing, what about the students and teachers? They too had to learn to speak other languages. Becoming a learner of mathematics, for example, involves learning to speak its language, to make "mathematical meaning." I became aware of the practical importance and theoretical significance of babbling math, babbling history, etc. in the students' performing as mathematicians, historians, poets, biologists, and so on. To learn mathematics developmentally, one needs to perform as a speaker of it without knowing how (Holzman, 1995). In this way (that is, methodologically), becoming a learner of "school subjects" is not so different from "baby" talk. Both are socially completive activities in which meanings are made.

The Institute closed the Barbara Taylor School in 1997. The school had been kept afloat through a modest tuition, grassroots fundraising by the Institute and parents, staff and friends of the school, and much volunteer labor. Even though students came from across the city, they were from working poor families who struggled to make their tuition payments. The school was financially unstable and there were no indications that that would change any time soon, either through increased donations or increased enrolment. Our unwavering commitment to nondidactic, noncognitive and collective learning was not an easy sell to parents who were being told by other schools that their children needed remedial programs and more homework and drills. Their reticence to take the risk with us was understandable, but unfortunate, and, in the last years, new students were primarily those who were having (and making) serious trouble in special education classes and special schools. That they blossomed at the Barbara Taylor School was no surprise to us, but we did not want to become a special school. All told, we felt we could not justify keeping the school open any longer. We had discovered and developed a lot. We would invest what we had learned in the further development of the outside of school programs that were being directed by colleagues familiar with our methodology, and which I will discuss in Chapter 4.

PLAYING WITH THE SCHOOL SCRIPT

In the decade plus since the Barbara Taylor School closed, my educated guess is that the need for learning environments like it has only increased. No small part of why I think so is what I see as a new "mass emotion" of fear surrounding education. Children, parents, teachers, principals, superintendents and politicians are frightened that they, their children, their classes, their schools, their districts and their cities are going to get failing grades. In more and more ways, people are organizing their lives around trying to prevent this from happening or covering up that it is happening. There are many signs of this disturbing cultural phenomenon: The proliferation and popularity among parents (across class lines) of Kaplan and other testing and remediation companies; the identi-fication of serious symptoms of stress among children as young as 6 around test time; the trend toward interviewing 3-year-olds for private school admission when they reach age 6; the widespread elimination of music, art, drama and physical education from the school curriculum (and more recent threats to eliminate history, as reported in ASCD Smart Brief, January 2008) to give more time for test preparation. Even as people are taking these actions, they worry that they are actually doing more harm than good, thus adding to their fear of failing. The catalyst for this emotional tidal wave was the enactment in 2002 of a new educational policy bill, No Child Left Behind (NCLB).

And yet, schooling was scripted in the USA (and elsewhere) long before NCLB. Sometimes the intense debate over the policy can make it seem otherwise. Some of its harshest critics give the impression that before NCLB came along, classrooms across the USA were hotbeds of creativity and spontaneity, and that the new mandated national assessment and accountability measures have taken that away. Of the many reasons I object to NCLB, this is not one of them.

Schools and classrooms have many scripts. There is the script of how teachers and students "do school" including the complex dynamics of race, class, language and culture (what was called in the 1970s and 1980s the "hidden curriculum"). As well, each school subject has its specific scripted curriculum. Much has been written about these scripts and the ways in which they perpetuate inequal-ity and constrain learning. The script that I am most interested in challenging, however, and that I believe Vygotsky's most innovative ideas about learning, development and play are relevant to, is the one that underlies and validates these other scripts. This "meta-script" is education's version of mainstream psychology's theory of human learning. Having mentioned aspects of this meta-script previously, here I bring them together. Learning is the acquisition of information (knowledge) and skills by discrete individuals. What and how an individual can learn at any given time is dependent on a number of factors and their complex interaction, the primary factor being the developmental level of that individual. The decades-old practice of separating students into homogenous groups (in primary schools entire classrooms and, within classrooms, reading and math groups, etc.) is based in this meta-script. So are the practices that comprise developmentally appropriate education. Testing itself is based in it, as is any type of individual assessment.

As far as I can tell, these practices are rarely questioned in the public outcry over NCLB. The critics point out how misguided and destructive the educational paradigm can be when carried to extremes, but they are not taking the opportunity to examine the shared constellation of beliefs, values and techniques underlying these and even more moderate school practices or calling for a paradigm shift. This leads me to believe that NCLB is not so much a radical departure from the norm as it is a logical extension of a very long-playing (badly written but intensely acted) school play, adapted many decades ago from psychology's flawed conceptual framework. It also reinforces my belief that what is needed is a radical break with schooling, but this will not happen in this conservative cultural climate. What I think can be done now is helping the people in school play – even if not in the extraordinarily developmental way very young children do.

In Chapter 2 I wrote about the social therapy weekend retreats in which participants created improvisational scenes ("performed their lifetimes") and their impact on the understanding and development of social therapy. From that point on, the Institute and organizations that shared our methodology began to use improvisation and become familiar with its tradition and how it was being used around the world. The addition of improvisation to my package of developmental learning concepts once again brought me both closer to and farther from Vygotsky's own work. It also led to the design of an educational intervention to bring "even a little development" into public school classrooms – environments in which the curriculum and the students' and teachers' actions are tightly controlled, and their fears are kept under control.

The broadest meaning of improvisation is "without preparation" or "spontaneous" and, in everyday talk, it is a common way people refer to having to deal with "the unexpected." In some discourses, being improvisational means "being present," and reacting to what is in one's immediate environment. When used this way (especially by people in management consulting and organization development), improvisation is understood as akin to and/or part of the processes of invention, creativity, innovation, generating ideas and creating new ways to be and to see. Musicians, dancers and actors often add the quality of performing instinctively to their understanding of improvisation.

Right off the bat, then, might we think of human life (indeed, human history) as one long improvisation? To me, improvisation is a way to characterize the being/becoming dialectic that is development. Planned as many cultures and individual lives might be, they are, in their totality, improvisational. It is the from-a-distance, after-the-fact accountings of events that make them appear anything but. Once I began playing around with improvisation from a socio-cultural, developmental psychology point of view, I realized that improvisation, as either a conception or an object of study, has historically been absent from discussions of culture, human development and education, and from psychology more broadly. While there are contemporary researchers who study improvisation, mostly in connection with creativity (Csíkszentmihályi, 1991; Göncü and Perone, 2005; Sawyer, 1997, 2001, 2003), the improvisational nature of human development throughout the life span is, I believe, a rich area for exploration.

The term "improv" has two common uses. One is as a shorthand for improvisation; the other is as the name of a particular theatrical genre and/or performance technique. Most commonly seen in comedy clubs or on TV ("Whose Line Is It Anyway?" is a popular UK- and US-syndicated TV show), improv is a performance art in which an ensemble of actors creates scenes or stories without a script (usually from audience suggestions). Improv is anchored in a small set of tools and techniques that allows the performers – by working off each other to create the stage, characters and plot – to go anywhere and make anything happen. As such, it is perhaps a unique kind of play, combining elements of pretend play, game play and theatrical play to create something other than any of them. To do improv (*play the game*) players need to follow the rules (no matter where their imagination might want to take them), but to do improv (*perform*) players need collectively to create the imaginary situation in such a way that the rules will emerge in their playing. Like pretend play, it has no end point or goal outside of itself; like game play, mastering the rules is essential to becoming skillful; and like theatrical play, it is played in front of an audience.

The basic rules of improv are simple to state but very difficult to master: *Accept offers and build with them* and *Don't negate*. An offer is anything that someone says or does – a shrug of the shoulder, a jump in the air, a verbal greeting, a threatening hand motion, a joyful noise, sitting still and silent. Accepting the offer can look a million different ways, but they don't include denying or disagreeing. For example, a two-person scene might begin with one person saying, "I love you." If the partner says, "Very good, Mr Kim. Your English is improving," she is not only accepting what is said (the offer) but building the scene with it (and making an offer to her partner). If she instead says, "I've never seen you before in my life" she would have negated the offer and made it more difficult to further the scene. Following these two rules is the basis for the often awe-inspiring comedic performances of highly skilled improvisers.

For me, the experience of watching, learning and teaching improv was simultaneously the experience of revisiting Vygotsky. I saw improv as a special kind of play that "plays" with rules and the imagination, the features Vygotsky identified as central to pretend and game play. I saw improv as a tool-and-result activity, in which the creating of the scene and the scene come into existence simultaneously. I saw improvisers as zpd creators, creating the "zone" for their social performance of going beyond what they know and know how to do. I saw improv as the socially completive activity of making meaning. I saw improv as bridging education's cognitive–emotive divide with its simultaneity of action and reflection and socially produced and shared thinking-and-feeling.

Outside of psychology there exists a literature on the value of improvisation and training in improv comedy techniques, which my coworkers and I became familiar with. Improv training for nonactors, which began its popularity in the 1990s, is said to enhance collaboration, confidence, attention, listening skills, spontaneity and creativity. Improv comedy troupes, like Second City in Chicago, have developed corporate training arms and begun to sell improv training to businesses. The precedent for doing improv games with children was set by Virginia Spolin who, as a settlement worker for the Works Progress Administration (WPA) Recreation Project in the 1930s, created what were essentially improv games as a kind of theater training that could cross ethnic and racial barriers. She subsequently formalized these into "theater games," founded the Young Actors Company (for children age 6 and up) in Hollywood in the 1940s, and had a successful career as a developer and practitioner of improv training. Spolin is revered in the "improv world" (and well known among drama teachers). Her books (*Improvisation for the Theater*, 1963; *Theater Games File*, 1975; and *Theater Games for the Classroom: A Teacher's Handbook*, 1986) made her approach to teaching and learning available to classroom teachers. But there is little evidence that her methods had a significant impact on classroom teaching, even during the 1970 and 1980s.

Throughout the 1990s and the first years of this century, close colleagues of mine were developing performance-based projects for inner-city youth outside of school (the All Stars Project, discussed in Chapter 4) and for corporate leaders and employees in the workplace (Performance of a Lifetime, discussed in Chapter 5). Newman also gathered together professionally trained actors who were working on these projects and formed an improv comedy troupe. At the Institute, we ran ongoing teacher supervision and offered "Improvisation for Teachers" workshops for several years. We also designed a few performance-based programs for children both in and after school, some of which became the subject of qualitative research studies (Feldman, in press; Holzman, 2000; Sabo, 1998). As a community we were gathering our own evidence that improvisation, as a type of performance, was a developmental learning activity for people of all ages.

While it was not realistic to ask public school teachers and students to perform/play school in the way we had with the Barbara Taylor School, we could at least invite them to play with the school scripts they were handed. Improvisation was a way to bring a performatory learning model into classrooms, a nondidactic teaching-learning method for experiencing learning as a social, creative process.

In 2006 the Institute began a program to train a small number of public school teachers in this approach. Headed by Rutgers University teacher educator Carrie Lobman, to date the program has graduated two classes of public and charter school preschool, primary and secondary school teachers. While she was a preschool teacher, Lobman trained in social therapy and also took improv classes for several years. She left teaching and went on to get her doctorate in early childhood education. Her research investigated the quantity and quality of early childhood teachers' "natural" improvisation. Along with other researchers, Lobman has drawn connections between teaching and performance and between expert teaching and improvisation (Baker-Sennett and Matusov, 1997; Borko and Livingston, 1989; Griggs, 2001; Lobman, 2003, 2005, under review; Pinaeu, 1994; Yinger, 1980, 1987). Sawyer (2004) has even called for the use of improvisation as the new metaphor for teaching. Lobman and others also point to similarities between improvisational teaching and the pretend play of young children, highlighting improvisation as a way that adults rediscover the creative and collaborative skills they had as children (Johnstone, 1981; Lobman, 2005; Lobman and Lundquist, 2007; Nachmano-vitch, 1990; Sawyer, 1997; Spolin, 1963).

The initial goals of the Institute's program, called the Develop-ing Teachers Fellowship Program, were to develop the creative and improvisational skills of the teachers, and to train them to see and relate to teaching and learning as performance and to their students as performance ensembles that have collective responsi-bility for creating their learning environment. We hoped that teachers and students would have some fun in the process, reduce their fear of failing and, overall, make going to school a bit more pleasant. During the year-long program, the teachers participated in bi-weekly workshops, in which conversations on creating devel-opmental learning through performance were weaved in and out of improv training. Teachers also had mentors who worked with them in their classrooms once a month. Teachers were also required to design and carry out a demonstration project for their school.

The 22 teachers who have gone through the program thus far have creatively adapted and transformed what they were learning. They invented new improv games and new situations in which to play them, introduced performance language to their students and taught them to be performance directors. They and their students played with creating new performances of themselves in their teacher and students roles.[6]

One teacher described how she and her students exaggerated their usual ways of behaving: "I have a hard time with authority, so I have been trying on a really over-exaggerated character of authority. Like a caricature of authority – I walk around. "No smiling! No laughing! I don't want to hear that! – which the students love and they really will behave differently for, because I play that and then they play the really super-exaggerated perfect students" (Lobman, in press).

Another teacher described one of her new "weird" performances:

> I feel that one of the ways I have grown from learning this approach is that I am willing to be weird in the classroom. On the one hand, as the inclusion teacher in two second grade classrooms it often falls to me to be the disciplinarian – to pull children aside and talk to them about what they are doing wrong. On the other hand, I believe that the scripts that teachers and children follow at those moments are very constraining and role-driven. So, I have started playing with that character and sometimes I walk up to children and give them the whole lecture about what they did wrong and why it was wrong . . . but I do it in gibberish. I say the whole thing in total gibberish. And then I walk away. It's been very interesting to see how the children respond to this – but one thing for sure is that they are no longer focused on whatever they were doing before.
>
> (Lobman, personal communication, 12 February 2008)

In general, the teachers have found that improv games help their students to be more cooperative and aware of how the action of an individual impacts the group, and give them opportunities to take risks and be creative in ways that extend beyond doing written tasks. They themselves, as teachers, were more able to be collaborators with their students and "removed from the role of the sole decision maker" (Lobman, personal communication, 12 February 2008).

The teachers used their training to improvise with the script of the official curriculum, adapting games they had learned or making up their own to use in teaching specific subjects and grade levels. As one example, a high school history teacher adapted *The Bus* (Lobman and Lundquist, 2007, p. 148) for use in her 9th Grade World History class. In *The Bus*, characters with different emotions come one by one onto the bus and everyone on the bus takes on the emotion of each new passenger and continues what they are doing and saying. They then lose these emotions one at a time as each passenger gets off the bus. The teacher created *The History Bus* as an improvisational activity to assess her students' understanding of the key historical figures they were studying. Students chose characters to be the passengers they would perform, and the scene began. In her write-up of this activity, the teacher commented:

> As the figures entered the bus, it was interesting to see their depth of understanding, even between figures that didn't live in the same time period. There was a verbal argument between Marie Antoinette and a Third Estate citizen hungry for bread; a discussion between Martin Luther and Jesus about what Jesus really intended for his followers; a disagreement between Martin Luther and the Pope, between Machiavelli and Pericles, and between Shi Huangdi and Voltaire.
>
> (Lobman, in press)

As this teacher and Lobman see it, this activity allowed the students to actively engage with the content of the world history curriculum and simultaneously required them to create with each other and with the teacher. While eight students "rode the bus" everyone in the class contributed to the performance by working to shape the characters. Students playing the characters were not put on the spot and students who did not perform as characters in the scene shared responsibility for the content. The curriculum was not only material to be learned, but also material for the creation of ongoing improvised performances. The teacher and the students discovered what historical content they knew by playing with it (Lobman, in press).

I heard about this experience when I was reading Jonathan Kozol's recent book, *The Shame of the Nation: The Restoration of Apartheid Schooling in America*. Near the end of the book, Kozol writes, "The schools where children and their teachers still are given opportunities to poke at worms, and poke around into the satisfaction of uncertainty . . . are the schools I call 'the treasured places.' They remind us always of the possible" (Kozol, 2005, p. 300). The phrase "satisfaction of uncertainty" is a beautiful one, capturing the unity of affect and cognition that is possible when children are learning to perform and performing to learn.

Chapter 4

Outside of school

Creatively imitating and incorporating the other

> Instead of selling my body, I dance.
>
> (15-year-old girl from Queens, NY, in
> All Stars Talent Show Network)

I am far from a big crier but every time I see young people singing, rapping or dancing on stage I get teary eyed. I cannot, and feel no need to, name the emotion but can only say that it is like no other. Their energy, concentration, boldness and letting the audience see how much they care about what they are doing moves me deeply. Showing that you care is not easy for anyone in the current culture, and it is especially hard for adolescents. Environments in which they can take this risk are, in my opinion, very special. To the extent that they exist, they tend to be created outside of school rather than in it – schools are too cognitively overdetermined to allow the activity of caring to flourish. For me, bringing Vygotsky to bear on children's lives outside of school means, in large part, providing opportunities for performances that are the unity of intellect and affect, performances of caring, interest, curiosity and passion.

Discussing how these opportunities are provided, and keeping Vygotsky in the conversation, is not an easy task. I want to share some of the programs developed from Newman's and my Vygotskian-inspired understanding/practice of performance as the tool-and-result activity of human development. In doing so, I offer my understanding of some of what makes it hard for youth to do their caring and curiosity socially. To provide context, I also want to summarize how the experts view the benefits of outside of school programs, especially performing arts programs, in relation to development and learning. But to do so is to bring together three areas of study, each with its own language, conceptual framework and agenda – after school and out-of-school time research and evaluation; the fields known as drama in education, theatre-in-education, and applied theatre; and work of Vygotskian-oriented scholars who look at after school learning environments. It is my hope that in bringing these areas into brief (and perhaps awkward) interface, I give a sense of the potentials and limitations of how outside of school programs are constructed and studied. I begin with this interface.

Dialogue and debate about children and adolescents is so often focused on the educational opportunities and roadblocks of schooling that it is easy to forget that they have learning lives outside of school. Young people in the USA spend only about 25% of their time in school (Heath, 2000, p. 34). Families with time and money are able to organize their children's out-of-school time to supplement school learning through trips, camps, organized sports, cultural and religious programs, and individualized lessons. Such is not the case for the majority of low-income and ethnic minority students. Beginning in the 1990s this difference between the more and the less privileged became an important area of investigation for educational researchers and developmental psychologists who realized that overidentifying education and learning with schooling was a mistake, and who were beginning to embrace the concept of *youth development*. Youth development represents a paradigm shift from viewing youth as problems to viewing them as resources, and from a prevention model to an approach that builds on their strengths and capabilities to develop as successful adults within their own community (National Collaboration for Youth, 1996, p. 1).

Two questions began to be asked: To what extent do outside of school educational and cultural enrichment activities contribute to school success; and what features of structured outside of school time foster youth development? Edmund Gordon and his colleagues coined the term *supplemental education* to characterize the varied enrichment experiences that lead to high academic achievement and foster the development of human and social capital. In their ongoing work, they delineate and advocate for research and changes in policy and family and community practice that will bring about universal access to such experiences (Bridglall, 2005; Gordon, 1999; Gordon *et al.*, 2005). (Another term in use is *complementary learning*, an initiative of The Harvard Family Research Project, http://www.gse.harvard.edu/hfrp/.)

Within this context, outside of school programs are being looked to as supplemental educational environments. At the same time, outside of school programs are being asked to show direct evidence that they lead to specific outcomes (such as higher test scores) and are under pressure to become more school-like by providing homework help and mirroring the school curriculum – which would make them not supplementary or complementary at all. This situation has contributed to a flurry of studies on outside of school programs and produced some findings relevant to socio-cultural, activity-theoretic, Vygotskian principles, particularly in relation to performance based and culturally oriented programs.

The benefits to children and adolescents of participating in outside of school cultural and performing arts programs have been evident to arts educators and theatre practitioners for decades. They and the young people who participate in their programs share informally and anecdotally stories of lives turned around, passions found and confidence gained. Researchers and evaluators have now added their voices. Findings from both large-scale quantitative and program-specific qualitative studies have found that theatre, performing arts and arts programs for young people are developmental in a variety of ways (e.g. Arts Education Partnership, 1999; Carnegie Council on Adolescent Development, 1992; Heath, 2000; Heath, Soep and Roach, 1998; Gordon, Bridglall and Meroe, 2005; Jones, 2003; Mahoney, Larson and Eccles, 2005). Among the documented benefits, some point to the zpd nature of performing arts programs, such as the positive change in young people's attitudes toward one another that emerge from learning and creating as a group; the opportunities that young people have to learn from and build positive relationships with successful adult professionals; and the extended engagement in process that characterizes such programs. (The zpd is not mentioned by these authors; it is, rather, something that I see in their reports.)

Vygotskian-influenced researchers who look at outside of school programs and/or performing arts activities have focused on the social nature of the learning that takes place in such programs. They utilize the notion of the zpd as a scaffold to characterize the types of adult guidance that function effectively to mediate the appropriation of cultural artifacts (e.g. Betts, 2006; Cooper, 2004; Klein, 2007; Penuel, 1998; Salmon, 1980). The most comprehensive and sustained study of this type is that of Michael Cole and the Distributed Literacy Consortium (Cole *et al.*, 2006), whose model after school program, the Fifth Dimension, was designed to boost academic achievement. The Fifth Dimension was developed with cultural-historical activity theory as both object of research and guide to practice (Brown and Cole, http://lchc.ucsd.edu/People/ MCole/browncole.html). In the program, which is housed in community centers, children play computer games and game-like activities assisted by adult staff and students enrolled in a fieldwork course at a local college or university. The Fifth Dimension is conceptualized both as a zpd for collaborative problem solving and use of mediational tools, and as the activity system of which it is a part (the university–community partnership, school district and community). An innovative instrumental tool for school improvement, it has been replicated in programs operating across the USA and in Denmark, Sweden, Spain, Mexico and Brazil (Cole *et al.*, 2006, pp. 160–167).

The youth development perspective takes a broader view. Rather than looking at outside of school programs in terms of academic achievement, it looks at how programs challenge and support young people to develop emotionally, socially, culturally, intellectually and as responsible citizens (e.g. Barton, Watkins and Jarjoura, 1997; Finn and Checkoway, 1995; Pittman and Cahill, 1991; Resnick, Harris and Blum, 1993). The kind of benefits youth development researchers are looking for include feelings of belonging and self-worth, experiencing close, positive relationships with others and mastery of social, emotional and intellectual challenges.

Within this youth development framework, the "playful and performatory Vygotsky" that I have glimpsed is beginning to appear. For example, in a study of community-based youth programs, Heath determined that the highest quality programs were those that gave youth opportunities to perform in new and different types of roles, not just on stage, but within the program itself, through which they came to see themselves as "capable of acting outside and beyond the expected" (Heath, 2000, p. 39). From the field of evaluation, Sabo Flores proposes that participatory evaluation is a youth development activity. In her examinations of youth-led and youth-run outside of school programs (Sabo, 2003; Sabo Flores, 2007), she cites the ways in which youth "move beyond their socially determined roles" and

become leaders within the program, performing as directors, board members, funders, researchers, evaluators, planners, etc.

. . . Evaluation environments should be created in which young people and adults relate to one another as performers. Together they can articulate scripts and improvise various evaluation roles. This self-conscious use of performance supports a kind of playfulness – a trying on and trying out.

(Sabo, 2003, pp. 17–23)

I conclude this selective review with some words about football. A few years ago I came across an article that, as far as I can tell, has not made it into the literature on outside of school time. The writer, Herb Childress, is an ethnographer. He spent a year observing students at a Northern California high school, following them as they went to classes and spent time in structured and informal activities after school. Childress summarized his findings in an essay he titled, "Seventeen reasons why football is better than high school" – but, as he says, "You can substitute 'music' or 'theater' or 'soccer' for 'football,' and everything I say will stay the same; so when I say that football is better than school, what I really mean is that even football is better than school" (Childress, 1998, p. 617). His 17 reasons encompass many of the benefits cited above, but his list also contains others that point to the performatory quality of youth development: teenagers are encouraged to excel, get to choose their own roles and are honored (the community comes out to see them); emotions and human contact are expected parts of the work; the unexpected happens all the time; repetition is honorable; and a public performance is expected (Childress, 1998). To me, this sounds like a learning-leading-development environment.

PERFORMING IDENTITY

Remember the paradox Newman came up against in doing psychotherapy – that he could talk about his inner life even though he did not believe there was any such thing? Being involved in the development of youth programs for many years, I realized I was confronting an analogous paradox – that even though I don't believe there is such a thing as identity, adolescence is (as developmental psychology texts say) a time of identity formation. Just as Vygotsky was of help in understanding the paradox of therapy talk, he is helpful in understanding the paradox of identity. And just as it was not his writings on psychotherapy that were enlightening, it is not his writings on adolescent development ["Dynamics and structure of the adolescent's personality" (Vygotsky, 2004b); "Imagination and creativity of the adolescent" (Vygotsky, 1994b)] that have been particularly illuminating to me. In both cases, it is, rather, his insistence that the human practice of continuously relating with and incorporating "the other" is what makes every human being learn and develop in the unique ways they do – and I have described how I see this most vividly in his analysis of language and of play. This was an attempt to escape from the philosophical–psychological dualisms of self and other, inside and outside, and permanence and change, and to articulate a dialectical relationship of unity of self-other, inside-outside, permanence-change.

When I think of identity within this framework, it seems an odd sort of thing that doesn't fit. People develop as speakers, players, feelers, learners, problem solvers, conceptualizers, perceivers, lovers, fighters, and many other things that they can (but may not) get more skilled at by continuing to relate with and incorporate the other. Or they can stop developing in these ways or lose these capacities altogether. Not so with identity. Conceptually, identity is not something people can get better or worse at; it is something people have. Once formed, it remains unchanged throughout a lifetime (and the "loss of identity" is considered a psychopathology). As permanence, identity is nondevelopmental. As I will try to show below, the activity of young people outside of school has given me a way to understand identity consistent with my Vygotskian developmental framework: As socially completive activity, identity is no longer odd. It is not formed but, like speaking, it is *per*formed. Continuing to develop as a person past childhood, then, would involve continuing to perform identity.[1]

The easiest place to perform identity is on the theatrical stage. Whether scripted or improvisational, theatre requires performers to create character, to use who they are to create someone other than who they are. The key phrase here is "use who they are," for actors on stage do not lose who they are; they are simultaneously their characters and themselves. James Gandolfino does not stop being James Gandolfino when he is playing Tony Soprano (just as 3-year-olds do not stop being themselves when they play superheroes). Performing gives the lie to the either/or paradigm of reality, the having to choose between permanence and change, between I and not I. It demonstrates that one is both permanent and changing, oneself and other than oneself. The experience/activity of performing identity on the stage can move people beyond identity as a construct by which to understand and relate to themselves.

To illustrate what I am suggesting about identity and performing on the stage, I present some first-person accounts from young actors participating in an outside of school theater program called Youth OnStage! (YO!) in New York City. YO! is a program of the All Stars Project, the environment-and-activity through which Newman, myself and our close colleagues have attempted to create spaces for developmental learning to flourish outside of schools.[2]

In 2005, YO! produced *Our City*, inspired by Thornton Wilder's *Our Town* (written in 1938, it is still the most frequently performed play in the USA). Instead of setting the play in Grover's Corners, New Hampshire in 1905, YO! set it in New York City in 2005. The cast of eight young student actors – inner-city young women and men, ages 14–21 – constructed the play with the support of YO!'s directors and a few other adult professionals. The cast read Wilder's play, watched a video of its most recent Broadway production, and discussed aspects of the play and of their own lives. They went out on the streets and into the subways instructed by YO!'s directors to observe people unlike themselves – with respect to age, gender, ethnicity and physicality – and bring them back to perform for each other.

Through a series of exercises, each young actor created anywhere from two to four characters. They then improvised scenes between the characters, for example, a white cop and a homeless man meeting in the park in the early morning hours, a middle-class white female and working-class African American male having an awkward conversation on the campus of Columbia University. In cases where the performances were stereotypical or shallow, the cast and directors found people who were like the embryonic characters and brought them in to talk with the cast and help them deepen their understanding of who these characters were (becoming). For example, a Saudi woman came to speak about arranged marriages, a Columbia University graduate came to talk about campus life, and a NYC policeman came to share what it is like to be a cop.

The improvised scenes were audio taped and transcribed. Over a 6-week period, the characters came to have lives, and relationships between them developed. The actors and directors discussed how the various characters and scenes related to each other. The directors then shaped the transcribed scenes into a script. The script was then brought back to the actors, who adjusted and reworked it (particularly the dialogue) into the final script. The resulting play, utilizing the structure of *Our Town*, enjoyed a sold-out 3-week run. (One and a half years later, the play was revived with a different cast and brought to high schools and colleges throughout the city.)

Approximately 6 months after the play closed interviews were conducted with the original cast about their history with YO! and their experience in creating *Our City*. Much of what they said in the interviews corroborates previous findings of young people taking risks in the theater and growing emotionally and socially from it. These young actors spoke about the challenges to their identity they experienced and their understanding of how they have grown from them. I have chosen comments from interviews with three of the actors: Francelli, Michael and Sita.[3]

Francelli, a 19-year-old Dominican American, played Ali, a young male Arab American grocery clerk from the Bronx, and Erica, a street wise African American from Bed-Stuy, Brooklyn – characters she created from people she saw in her neighborhood.

> Playing Ali and Erica really helped me explore me as a person, my values. They helped me think different. And it challenged me as an actress, because literally from one minute to the next, I had to change from a man to a woman. Even though Erica had some of the same experiences as me, she was really outside of who I am. I'm a really nice person, and she's really not! . . . As an actress, it became difficult, because I was so connected to these characters, because so much of me was in them, I had to find a way to disconnect me from the character and just become that character. I learned a lot from them, they gave me a lot. Ali, for example. I would sit on the train and think like Ali – watching people. I already did that, but I did it more in depth because I was doing it as someone else, as Ali. I'd sit on the train, I'd watch people, I'd talk to people, to strangers. I would see NY through Ali's eyes, I would think the way he thinks, talk the way he talks. And when I would switch into Erica, I would walk down the street like I was a million dollars and I would ignore people. I really got into these characters

and this show helped me to develop and grow not just as an actress but as a person.

Michael, a 19-year-old African American, played Jack, a white cop, and Isaiah, a young African American street and subway musician (bucket drummer). (Jack was created out of a white cop who had recently given Michael a ticket for dropping his Metrocard on the subway platform.)

> I have to say *Our City* was one of the most challenging and the most interesting things that I've ever done in my life. Why? Because we had to portray characters who were completely not us. . . . Performing is all about creating someone who's not you. It's an art. It's like drawing; you have a big canvas that you want to fill with these different things, different feelings, different experiences. Drawing a character is like drawing a picture. But I wasn't drawing it by myself; we were all working together. Working together as a team, as one, putting all the lines together, even though we all had different characters, putting all the lines, and all these minds, together. It was fun for us. No one ever missed a rehearsal. The vibe was just so beautiful; everyone was just so up for it.

Seventeen-year-old Sita, who moved to New York from Bangladesh when she was two years old, created and performed three characters: a 74-year-old African American woman from Brooklyn, a 50ish overweight, Irish-American high school teacher from Staten Island, and a teenage Saudi Arabian bride-to-be visiting the Bronx to meet her arranged fiancé.

> Whatever I held onto as Sita got in the way of being Drumgoolie or the Black grandmother or the Arabian bride. I'm not allowed to be Sita and it's just as simple as that – that's the great thing about theater, you break free from those things. Who you are doesn't matter anymore . . . I learned that people change and they're not what you expect them to be so don't expect. Let them act and then, you know, converse with them. The way I started my characters turned out to be completely different by the time I was done. And I realized that people develop even in fake worlds – people do develop – and I was not expecting that . . . I owe theater a lot and acting,

performing, for letting me be who I am now. I'm definitely more open. As far as who I think I am goes, I keep my options open. I don't let myself believe one thing or the other. It's not black or white. I see different shades and I see different colors and I'm letting those colors go wild. I'm not going to limit myself anymore. There's definitely more to me. And I see that now.

I was struck by how the young people spoke about their experiences and themselves in terms more artistic, cultural and emotional than evaluative or cognitive ("having a big canvas," "letting those colors go wild"). The interviews also showed me something about the difference between doing what you do not know how to do as a young child and as a teen or young adult. Francelli, Michael and Sita relate to the new things they are doing as different from and even discontinuous with their current lives, as challenges to who they have come to think they are. I see this in the interview excerpts above, and also in some of their comments on aspects of YO! other than performing their characters. They spoke of putting aside petty fights in order to work as an ensemble and learning to act as professionals, but perhaps the most telling statement was Michael sharing with the interviewer that just coming into Manhattan was hard for him. He continues, "I had never done that before in my life. Every time I came to the city before was with my family. It was a challenge for me to do something different, to come into the city to do something that I loved doing."

IF YOU CAN PERFORM ON STAGE, YOU CAN PERFORM IN LIFE

In addition to YO!, the All Stars Project (out of its performing arts complex on 42 St, in the heart of New York's commercial theater district) runs three other development programs for young people, the majority from poor and working-class communities, and provides training and organizational support to those wishing to start All Stars programs in their communities, both in the USA and internationally. In the New York City metropolitan area, the All Stars programs annually involve thousands of young people, ages 5–25, in different activities that invite them to perform their lives, both on and off stage. The All Stars staff is aided by hundreds of adult volunteers – both trained professionals and "ordinary" people from all walks of life. Some volunteers work directly with the programs and others raise the funds that make the programs possible. The All Stars takes no government funds and raises millions of dollars annually through a unique fundraising model that reaches out to individuals of all income brackets for financial support, and first-hand involvement if they wish.

As I have watched, participated in and studied the All Stars since its beginnings two decades ago, I have come to believe that the participation of so many adults on a voluntary basis and as financial donors contributes equally, if not more, to the development of the young people as does the content of the programs. In Vygotskian and activity theory terms, these adults are an element of the overall socio-cultural ecology or activity system (Cole *et al.*, 2006), a specific sort of intergenerational participation in the social formation of individual development. I would add that they immeasurably increase the possibilities for creating many and varied zpds, overlapping and interacting throughout the system.

Many of the young people who participate in the All Stars could tell a story similar to Michael's of rarely leaving their neighborhoods – neighborhoods in which they say, "There's nothing to do." Over US$1 billion is spent annually to provide after school care in the USA through the federally funded 21st Century Community Learning Centers (Bodilly and Beckett, 2005). Philanthropies, cultural institutions and community organizations spend millions more. Presumably, there are after school programs even in the poorest of neighborhoods. How do young people view these programs? Comments from a focus group of All Stars volunteers and participants provide some insight (Holzman, 2002). Their impressions of most programs were that they are for special populations ("You have to be pregnant or in a gang to get into them") and that this was because of how they are funded ("They get money from the government to help this group or that group"). The All Stars, in contrast, is open to anyone ("The money comes from ordinary people and it's used for ordinary people").[4]

I would not have thought that young people were aware of the funding and staffing aspects of programs set up to serve them. Perhaps most are not and it is the unusual nature of the All Stars that made these particular young people notice. What I take from their observations is that they have an awareness of the total environment in which they are related to by adults – the total All

Stars environment and the social-political-economic environment of their community and the broader culture (of which the All Stars environment is a part). They recognize that nothing about the All Stars was imposed by Washington, D.C. or a funding body; that entry into a program is not based on being labeled as a certain kind of kid; and that the adults they work with are there because they want to be with them. The young people are, and feel like they are, builders of the programs and this gives them a whole new sense of who they are and what is possible for them.

"If you can perform on stage, you can perform in life." This is the mantra of Pam Lewis, the All Stars' director of youth programs. She shouts this message out from high school auditorium stages during Saturday sessions of the All Stars Talent Show Network (ASTSN), the oldest and largest of the organization's youth programs. Now in her 40s, Lewis seized the opportunity to lead the ASTSN shortly after coming to New York City from Kansas. An actor and singer who grew up in a middle-class African American family, Lewis was also a political activist, first inspired by the anti-apartheid movement and then by multiracial efforts to transform the political culture in the USA through independent electoral politics. Bringing performance to poor inner-city youngsters became a way for her to bring together what she felt on a gut level – the transformative power of performing on stage – and what she knew intellectually – that Americans, including its young people of color, did not have political change on their social agendas.

The ASTSN grew in the mid 1980s and was influenced by Newman's and my emerging understanding/practice of performance as the tool-and-result activity of human development in social therapy and education. Its founders wanted to do something positive in the face of the failure of schools to educate African American and Latino children and the lack of enrichment activities in their neighborhoods. Once they reach school age, children have few environments in which they can be creative, and fewer where they can be creative on their own terms. Music and dance is one of these environments and, within the African American community, talent shows are a part of the culture. Could we use the phenomenon of talent shows to "exploit" young people's love of performing on stage for their own overall development and that of their communities? The idea was to hold neighborhood talent show auditions in which everyone who auditioned made it into the show, participated in improvisational performance workshops, and had the responsibility of building the audience for the day of the show. This was the design for connecting performing on stage with performing in life.

The ASTSN involves young people, ages 5–25, in producing and performing in talent shows that are held in high schools throughout the city in mostly poor Black and Latino neighborhoods. When the program began more than 20 years ago, the auditions, workshops and show were held in church basements and community centers in poor communities. As it grew larger, high school auditoriums were the only neighborhood venues large enough to accommodate the large crowds. Now the workshop sessions take place at the All Stars' headquarters in Manhattan. This difference in location means that hundreds of children and teens leave their neighborhoods and come into Manhattan to do something they have never done before. This is a big step for many, many of them. The children and teenagers perform on stage solo, in twos, threes or dance groups of more than twenty, usually of mixed ages. Others work side-by-side with adult theater professionals and peer volunteers on every aspect of the production: sound, lights, cues, stage-managing, ushering, safety, security, registration, and so on. Former performers who become volunteers also recruit and mentor younger children from their neighborhoods, bringing new acts and new volunteers to the next cycle. A typical show brings out 200–400 young people to the audition and workshop segments of the talent show cycle. At the actual show (usually 3 weeks later) they perform in front of audiences of 800–1500 people, family and friends who have bought tickets from the performers.[5]

The experience of going through the cycle and performing on stage in front of an audience of friends and strangers is profound for many of these young people (on a survey about the program, one 11-year-old girl wrote, "I thought I couldn't do anything"). Many of those who participate in a show remain active with the All Stars beyond one show or return to it some time in the future. These veteran All Stars credit the program with keeping them off the streets and out of trouble, being positive, "staying focused," learning how to have conversations with adults, and "becoming a leader instead of a statistic."

In its early years, the ASTSN was thought of and promoted as a positive alternative to violence and gangs – a program that gives young people something to do that they get recognition for and something to belong to. While it surely remains that, today the ASTSN is described as a development program, a description that I think it has grown into and which I prefer for several reasons. First, it suggests the psychology of becoming that underlies the program's mission. Second, it removes any hint of the program having a problem-solution orientation. More broadly, it minimizes misunderstanding that the program's mission is to boost academic achievement. And third, it opens the door to conversations about performance and development with the young people coming into the programs, their families, volunteers and donors. As I understand it, the ASTSN is a zpd- and culture-creating activity involving people of different ages and cultural/ethnic backgrounds, at differing levels of development, experience and skill, in creating stages on which young people can "make their statement" and in the process experience themselves as successful and as ensemble producers of things – and have their families and broader community share these experiences. It is a tiny step beyond identity and a little taste of what Pam Lewis means by performing in life.

NEW STAGES

In addition to YO! and the ASTSN, there are two other All Stars' youth programs: the Joseph A. Forgione Development School for Youth and the Production of Youth by Youth. Like many outside of school programs those of the All Stars aim to expose young people to more of the world. Enrichment activities – whether focusing on different cultures and customs, science, technology, sports or the arts – are designed to spark their interests and give them opportunities to discover and develop their talents. As important as these goals are, they are secondary for the All Stars, which sees the need for young people to become more worldly as the priority developmental issue.

This is especially the case for poor children and children of color, like the ones who participate in All Stars' programs. For far too many of them, their world is the projects (public housing) and the street corner. Nineteen-year-olds who have never taken a subway ride into the city by themselves, have never traveled except to visit relatives, have never seen live theatre, have never worn a suit except to go to funerals or court appearances are common in one of the most cosmopolitan cities in the world (and, no doubt, other urban poor communities). Their lack of worldliness is an outgrowth of the smallness that racism, classism, segregation and poverty produce. There are hundreds of ordinary ways of relating in the world that most children and adolescents who come from very poor communities are not exposed to; they feel uncomfortable outside their neighborhoods because they don't know the social conventions of how to participate. They feel unwelcome and they are, because those who are strangers to them are equally uncomfortable. The All Stars has used performance to develop a methodology to intervene on this cultural deprivation. Neither glorifying nor rejecting black culture or youth culture, its programs help young people to be culturally cosmopolitan, more worldly and more sophisticated – which is to be more of who they are and more of who they are not.

This brings us back to the issue of identity and what I mean by performing or playing with identity in order to get outside or beyond it. Identity is a form of (unintentional) resistance or reticence to becoming worldly or sophisticated. We all respond with our identities, sometimes with awareness – entering a foreign country and have a sudden realization of, "Oh, I'm an American/Korean/African/European" – and sometimes not – pulling our arms closer to our bodies when rowdy teenagers enter a public space. All of us are also constrained by our identities at different times and places and to varying degrees, uncomfortable or fearful of doing something that would be out of character. Having a fixed identity can be particularly conservatizing for young people, especially poor, immigrant and youth of color – it can put the brakes on life's journey. I look at the All Stars' performance methodology as a particular response to the development and learning crisis of poor and minority urban youth and their communities: it is an attempt to support all around youth development, which entails young people becoming more worldly and culturally cosmopolitan, which requires minimizing the constraining effect of identity on incorporating the other.

Lenora Fulani has been a significant figure in the development of this methodology and message. She is an outspoken and controversial African American political activist (she was the first African American to be on the Presidential ballot in all 50 US states) and developmental psychologist. When Fulani cofounded the All Stars she lent her skills and experiences to Newman's and my efforts to create a psychology of becoming. She shaped the Development

School for Youth in its early years. (Fulani and I met in the late 1970s at Michael Cole's laboratory at the Rockefeller University; we have been friends and colleagues ever since.) She has strong opinions about being black in white America, as can be seen in this excerpt from her essay in *America Behind the Color Line* (Gates, 2004):

> We live in a country where it's about superiority and inferiority. The white experience is seen as superior, the black experience as inferior, and most American institutions were developed for the superior people. Even things that have nothing to do with racial issues are seen in black and white. There is a sense in our communities that there is black behavior and there is white behavior. . . . White kids are insiders. They view themselves as insiders; they're connected to the American mainstream. Our kids feel like outsiders because they are, and you have to deal with that.
>
> (Fulani, 2004, pp. 107–108)

Performance, she believes, is how to deal with it. "A lot of the performances black kids currently have, they think of as the essence of themselves as black people. But they can learn a different way to perform, like they learn anything else" (Fulani, 2004, p. 104). When she trains adult professionals who volunteer to work with the young people,

> I tell them to teach the kids to be white, and they almost fall off their chair [out of fear that they will] step on their cultural toes. I tell them, believe me, they'll still be black. But why don't you use this time as an opportunity to share with them some of the secrets of white success and help them succeed in your world, given that your world is where we all wind up having to work? 'White' here is code for middle class, for upper middle class, but it's also code for moving beyond how many of us in these neighborhoods think of ourselves.
>
> (Fulani, 2004, p. 116)

   This kind of challenge to traditional concepts of identity is central to the Development School for Youth (DSY) and the Production of Youth by Youth (PYBY). Started in 1997, the DSY is a 13-week leadership-training program for 16- to 21-year-olds led by volunteer senior executives from corporations and law firms who introduce the students to the worlds of finance, culture, communications and other leading industries.[6] The program was conceptualized to directly engage donors from the business community in a unique partnership dedicated to the development of poor youth. According to All Stars president and CEO Gabrielle Kurlander:

> With the DSY, we were developing a new, non-instrumental model of philanthropy. Donors do not give money so that development can be brought to poor communities. Rather, the model is, by design, developmental for everyone who parti-cipates in our unique partnership: our donors and the target populations we serve, most primarily poor and minority youth, are all engaged in developing as they are creating something new together. We are creating new conversations between very divergent cultures.
>
> (Kurlander, 2008, personal communication)[7]

Founded in 2005, PYBY is a 4-month program introducing high school students to the world of cultural production. Adopting some of the elements of the DSY model and adding others specific to the cultural industries, the program consists of workshops led by theatre, television and music producers, museum curators and gallery owners; site visits to see how theatre, television, music and the graphic arts are produced and distributed; and the production of their own cultural forum. DSY graduates are placed in paid summer internships, PYBY graduates in 8-week unpaid internships.

The adults who work with the programs and observers like myself can see that the young people are grappling with their unworldliness, identities and assumptions about themselves and others. When the young people are asked in the course of a day how they are doing and how the program is going, they are open about ways they think they are changing. Occasionally they are asked to give feedback more formally through focus groups or a survey.

One thing that these young people share is what I have referred to as the "that-ness" of learning-leading-development – making the discovery not only of how to do what they do not know how to do, but equally important, *that* they can do it. An 18-year-old male graduate of DSY commented, "I realized I am more than a Black kid from Brooklyn and that I could do good things and make a better life." A 17-year-old female from PYBY shared her discovery, "Meeting these producers changed how I see things. To tell you the truth, I thought these things were impossible for me. It gave me a little bit of hope that dreams can come true."

Some of the young people were specific about how they saw themselves changing. An 18-year-old aspiring male fashion designer said,

> I learned the distinction between confidence and arrogance. I was shy, but I was sort of arrogant. I learned from doing this, from meeting a lot of the people we met, that I didn't know as much as I thought, that being a designer was more complicated than I thought. Somehow, I don't know how, that made me less arrogant, but more confident.

A 19-year-old female DSY graduate shared this self-observation, "Before I wouldn't really go out of my comfort zone. Now I'm finding myself doing that a lot. When I start getting too comfortable I try to challenge myself." Another DSY graduate had this to say, "I saw the world as a chaotic place to live. I always looked down on the world. Now I embrace it and am proud to live."

The young people also spoke about being exposed to different kinds of people. They frequently contrasted the All Stars programs with their school, for example, "I met so many different people and learned of so many different cultures. My school is predominantly black and I don't learn about other cultures but here I do." They shared what they took away from these meetings and what they learned about people. "I met people who followed their passions, and they made it"; "Everyone I know, they do the same thing. Even all the grown ups, they do the same thing as everyone else they know. Before, I didn't know anyone who did special things, different things, like the producers"; "I thought they wouldn't let me past the front desk. But they were very friendly and interested in us"; and "There are positive people around and it makes me want to act like them."

At the beginning of this chapter I shared my understanding that making Vygotsky's insights relevant to life outside of school means giving children and adolescents opportunities to do what they rarely can do in school, which is to engage in social performances of caring, interest, curiosity and passion (performance that give expression to the unity of intellect and affect). Learning and development in early childhood are these kinds of social performance, in large part, because they are not cognitively overdetermined. The preschool learning-leading-development environment (the zpd) is jointly created for playful and improvisational performances of speaking, listening, eating, dressing, story telling, and so on. Creating these performance spaces and performances, I have said, involves the ongoing interplay of creative imitation and completion, which is my accounting for how it is that human beings do what we do not know how to do and learn and grow from that activity. I also have characterized this interplay as "incorporating the other." People become who they are through others. This is my elaboration of the Vygotskian claim that learning and development are fundamentally social activities.

It is, apparently, relatively easy and painless to incorporate the other in early childhood – that is, before there is a well-formed "I." Incorporating the other after "I" is a different activity because there is now an "I" who is doing it. Doing what you do not know how to do now involves awareness that there is a you who does not know how to do it. Creatively imitating and allowing others to complete for you involves a decision to do so on some level. *Playing/performing now includes the element of playing/performing with your sense of self.* It seems to me that these new developments are important to take into account in understanding not only how it is that outside of school programs typically are more effective learning environments than school but also how they foster youth development.

As I look at outside of school programs with this perspective, I see the All Stars programs I just described as environments designed in such a way that school-aged children and adolescents can play/perform with their sense of themselves and in the process (decide to) creatively imitate and incorporate the other, and become more worldly. This process of becoming worldly looks very different from what very young children do as they become worldly (or what developmental psychologists since Piaget call "learn about or acquire conceptions of the world"). Methodologically, however, preschool and school-aged children are actively playing with who they are and who they could be. I think that all developmental outside of school activities are performatory in this sense. Performance looks one way on the football field. It looks another way in a youth participatory evaluation. Were I to observe a Fifth Dimension or other innovative and effective after school program, I suspect I would see performance and it would look yet another way.

The common expression, "Children are our future" bothers me. I recognize it is well intentioned, but I always hear it as separating "becoming" from "being" and relating to young people more as passive recipients of what adults create than as creators. Human history – past, present and future – is not age-related. Adults and children create culture together. To the extent that adults forget this, children may, unfortunately, turn out to be our future.

Chapter 5

At the workplace

Looking at ourselves

> The fundamental insight of twentieth century physics has yet
> to penetrate the social world: *relationships are more
> fundamental than things.*
>
> (Senge *et al.*, *Presence: An Exploration of Profound
> Change in People, Organizations and Society*, 2005,
> p. 193, original emphasis)

Like – and unlike – All Stars' Pam Lewis who tells inner-city youth
that if they can perform on stage they can perform in life, Cathy
Rose Salit invites "high-performing" corporate executives, middle
managers, financial analysts and Olympic athletes to get on stage
and perform. Salit, an accomplished singer, actor and improvisational comic, is conveying a similar message as Lewis, adapted from
Newman's and my understanding/practice of performance as the
tool-and-result activity of human development. She leads workshops for multinational corporations and organizations, working
with successful business professionals, not inner-city poor and
ethnic minority children and youth. Salit was at those weekend
social therapy retreats where Newman experimented with performance that I described in Chapter 2. She and Newman have been
friends and political colleagues for many years and after the retreats
he asked her to work with him to create a new project, which they
dubbed Performance of a Lifetime, Interactive Growth Theatre.
The idea was to create a stage for nonactors to perform improv-
isationally and experience its therapeutic effects. Those people who
signed up would get together once weekly for four weeks, create an
improvisation play and perform it in front of a paying audience.

From 1996 to 1999, approximately 400 people participated in
these sessions (with 2000 more attending as audience members). A

small but steady stream of "satisfied customers" asked if Performance of a Lifetime (POAL) would come to their workplace and
lead a workshop to help with tensions, teamwork or diversity
challenges. POAL complied. With dozens of organizational performance trainings under their belt, and in recognition that
business was more responsive to their product than were individuals, in 2000 the company turned its full attention to the corporate world, which is the stage upon which, as president of
POAL, Salit performs today.

Even though POAL no longer conducts interactive growth
theater sessions open to the public, its work with organizations still
contains the key elements of that model: (a) talking to participants
in the language of the theater as a necessary component of creating
a performatory environment; (b) using the "authority" of the stage
to give participants the license to do something quite out of the
ordinary, broadening each person's notion of "what you're allowed
to do"; and (c) letting them experience themselves as producers of
their relational activity and improvisers of new social relations.

POAL, along with Second City Communications in Chicago (the
corporate arm of the famed Second City improv comedy troupe),
was a pioneer in bringing the tools of theatre and improvisation to
business. This kind of work has expanded in the last decade, as
many businesses shift from a hierarchical, top–down organizational
structure to a more horizontal one comprised of work teams, and as
more actors and improv troupes open training and consulting firms
(Friedman, 1999, 2003; Nissley, Taylor and Houden, 2004). With
this expansion, and the assumption that improvisation is a model
activity fostering team building and creativity, has come scholarship
linking organizational activity and theatrical activity, something I
welcome. I was already convinced of the value of improvisational
performance – as the way adults can come closest to the kind of
freedom from environmental constraints ("reality") that Vygotsky
identified in the free (rule-and-result) play of young children – so
adding organizational development (or organizational studies) to
therapy, education and youth development was a logical extension.

The benefits of improvisation cited most often in the academic
literature and by consultants are: learning to think on your feet, to
be extemporaneous, to respond quickly to the unforeseen and
unpredictable, and to "think outside the box" (Sawyer, 2000; Vera
and Crossan, 2004). POAL would agree and so do I. However, I
think that POAL adds another dimension to the benefits of

bringing improvisation into organizations. To the monologic it adds the *dialogic*, to the individualistic it adds the *relational*, to the tool for result it adds *tool-and-result*, to the reactive it adds the *generative*, and to the acquisitional it adds the *developmental*. What it points to and supports is people exercising their capacity to not only respond creatively to the unforeseen but to *generate* the unforeseen.

This dimension has been noted by others speaking different discourses than mine. For example, organizational development consultant and jazz pianist Frank Barrett likens improvisation in conversation to the "aesthetic of attunement" cultivated by jazz improvisers – a commitment "to stay engaged with one another, to listen to emerging ideas and to pay attention to cues that can point to an unexpected trajectory" (Barrett, 2006, pp. 275, 276). To organizational psychologist Karl Weick, in improvisation "creation and interpretation need not be separated in time, and sense-making rather than decision making is embodied in improvisation" (Weick, 2000, p. 291). In an article entitled, "The complexity of improvisation and the improvisation of complexity: Social science, art and creativity," Alfonson Montuori discusses ways that the practice of improvisation poses challenges to traditional ways of thinking about social science, organization, action and subjectivity. I particularly resonated with this observation: "Life in a complex world, and a life which reflects and values the complexity of *both* self and world, requires the ability to improvise – to deal with, and indeed to create, the unforeseen, the *surprise*" (Montuori, 2003, p. 240). Creating the surprise in social relationships and in the conversations that both produce and reflect them requires seeing and hearing what the environment offers.

When I first turned my attention to POAL and others who brought improvisation to organizations in 2000, I framed my interest in the following (obviously rhetorical) series of questions:

> If Vygotsky is right, and performing is how we learn and develop, then don't the "living organizations", "learning organizations" and "passionate organizations" that business leaders are now speaking about need to recognize themselves as "performing organizations"? If creativity and growth come into existence when people together create zpd's in the home, the school, the theater, the ball field and the therapy office, can management and employees learn to create them at the

workplace? If getting up on a stage puts you in touch with your "performing self", teaches you that you can always create new performances of yourself and has been shown to help adults, teens and children create better functioning and happier families and peer groups, might it not do the same for teams and workgroups?

(Holzman, 2006, p. 261)

In that article I answered in the affirmative and still do today. However, I had overlooked a significant difference between the workplace and those other environments – while they are designed to help, develop, teach or otherwise occupy people in meaningful personal and/or social activities, the workplace is not. Firms, industries, corporations and institutions hire people to work; employees serve organizations and to the extent that services are provided to employees it is to keep them there and/or help them to be more productive. Learning and/or development is either collateral (as when individuals happen to learn new skills and/or develop socially or in other ways) or instrumental (as when management decides some skill upgrading or culture change is required). In both cases, the company's financial success or institution's continued existence is primary.

It is helpful to recognize this feature of work environments when bringing Vygotsky's conceptions or overall method to workplace and organizational studies. Business and industry are far more receptive to new ideas in learning theory, group dynamics and communication theory than are the fields of education and mental health. While schools continue to maintain an organizational model adapted from industry at least a century ago, industry has moved on. This is reflected as much in how employees (and students) are related to as it is in their respective physical environments and cultural climate. The trend in business is toward greater flexibility, worker autonomy, collaboration and creativity. The trend in education is the opposite. Business leaders speak in the discourses of emergence, complexity and multiplicity, and the gurus among them exhort the necessity of putting the emotional, artistic and social dimensions of human (labor) power to work to get the job done.[1]

Within this broad cultural shift in organizational design and practice, the Vygotskian concepts I have been discussing – learning as social, play, and the improvisational, performatory nature of zpds – are prominent. Far more than institutionalized education, psychology or youth development, business invests in collaborative learning strategies, recognizes the value of play and the need to bring work and play closer together, replaces the machine metaphor with a theater metaphor, and experiments with what creativity and improvisation consultants can bring to them. The results appear positive, judging from the organizational studies literature and the steadily increasing industry demand for training in these areas. My own research, which includes helping to shape and to study one of these consulting firms (POAL), is corroborative. How I think about it now is that the workplace can be a zpd-creating environment precisely because the focus is not on employees as individuals but, rather, on the organization (the group). To the extent that individual employees learn and/or develop it is through the process of collectively transforming the organization (the totality) and not themselves (particulars). The advent of the learning organization (Senge, 1990; Senge *et al.*, 1994; Renesch and Chawla, 2006), the improvisational organization (Drucker, 1988; Sawyer, 2003; Vera and Crossan, 2004; Weick, 2000) and the playful organization (Schrage, 1999) lends support to my belief that the individualistic bias of psychology and education is terribly misguided and a major contributor to the failure of institutionalized education, and that these institutions can learn something from organizations and organizational studies.

Another advance business has made is its acceptance of process. Ironically, it is business – the socio-cultural institution that creates and extols *products* – that has recognized how important it is to pay attention to *process*. Academic articles and mass market books insist that in order for organizations to compete in today's market, they and their people need to focus as much on the process by which products (both material and ideational) come into being as the finished product. In graduate schools of business, aspiring CEOs and managers are told that organization, knowledge and learning are all emergent; things and relationships are not only what they appear to be at the moment, they are also what they were and what they can become.[2] The idea is that when employees (in most cases, managerial) are more attuned to the creative process, they become more actively creative and productive. (Whether all this has trickled down to line workers, janitors, mail clerks, etc. is another question.)

POAL helps employees become more attuned to the creative process, and its clients are very satisfied with the results of the training and consulting services they receive. What interests me, however, is the developmentally therapeutic aspect of POAL's work, that is, how improvisation and performance are activities in and by which emotional-social development is created. I worked very closely with POAL during 2000–2001, the initial years during which it was piloting and fine-tuning its basic organizational training workshop, mostly with startup dotcoms and service-providing organizations. I functioned primarily as an inside qualitative researcher, an observing member of the training workshop team and leader of postworkshop supervisory sessions with employees. Although this was not my first professional experience with organizational clients (I had done a few years of qualitative market research for multinational corporations), it gave me a new view of workplace culture and its limitations and possibilities as a developmental learning environment. Today POAL has a portfolio of diverse products, including improvisational-based training, role-plays, and live and video vignettes. As compared to the earlier years, its clients tend to be established global companies who want advanced training for their top-level analysts, managers and salespeople.[3] I remain a close colleague and informal consultant.

To explore the developmentally therapeutic in POAL's approach to improvisation I will focus on two of its activities: The "Yes, and" exercise that is part of all improv training, and the 1-minute performance of a lifetime that is unique to POAL.

IMPROV AS A CONVERSATIONAL ZPD

In Chapter 3 I discussed how I see improv in Vygotskian terms: (a) as a tool-and-result activity, in which the creating of the scene and the scene come into existence simultaneously; (b) as a bridging of the cognitive–emotive divide with its simultaneity of action and reflection and socially produced and shared thinking-and-feeling; and (c) as the socially completive activity of making meaning. I described the principles of improv by which improvisers create their stage, characters and plot by working off each other: "Don't negate" and "Accept the offer and build with it." Expanding on these principles here, improv talk can be analogized to conversations (language games) with very young children. Adults accept the child's babble ("ba-ba") and complete it ("Yes, it's time for your bottle," "Uh oh, you dropped your bottle, I'll get it for you"). They don't negate or criticize, but rather accept the offer and build with it.

With babies, adults seem to do this kind of improvisational, conversational meaning making unaware. The same adults, however, are just as likely to respond to an adult, both at home and at work, by refusing the offer as by accepting it (and with equal unawareness). What passes for ordinary discourse is nothing like baby talk or improv. In everyday conversation people negate each other all the time and compete rather than complete. From an article by Blantern and Anderson-Wallace comes this workplace example, an instance of what the authors refer to as "the current conversational architecture" (Blantern and Anderson-Wallace, 2006, p. 74): "A: Did you take the instruction sheet down to Production? B: Why? A: Did you take it; yes or no? B: What if I did? A: Did you? B: There's no need to be so aggressive" (p. 75).

One of the values of bringing improv to the workplace is its potential to impact on conversation, not only to minimize such unpleasant exchanges but also to give people a method to transform it into something closer to the creative meaning-making activity it is with babies (but in an adult- and workplace-appropriate manner). This is exceedingly difficult for adults to do with any consistency. To get good at it requires a lot of practice, not only in speaking but also in listening, because in ordinary conversations, including those at the workplace, people tend to listen very selectively to what others are saying – to hear something they agree or disagree with, to assess the "truth value" of what is said, to size up the speaker and try to figure out what she or he "really" means, to plan a comeback, to hear the pause that signals "it's my turn now" – or all of the above.

"Yes, and" exercises are the main way improvisers practice listening. POAL designs these exercises consistent with Newman's and my understanding of speaking and listening as social completive activity (rather than as representational of outer reality or expressive of inner thoughts or feelings). A goal of POAL's work is to help participants develop the ability to approach workplace conversations of any sort as improvisational scenes in which they have the responsibility to keep the scene going. This is a paradigm shift, on a sensuous, bodily and affective level, from person-to-person communicating to relational meaning making. Speaking, in this sense, can be thought of not as a telling of what is

going on but as a creating of what is going on, where understanding each other comes about through this relational activity.

Skilled improvisers have little difficulty keeping a scene going
because they hear and see offers everywhere – in a twitch, a frown,
even a silence. In contrast, brand new improvisers, if they see or
hear offers at all, see and hear the big, obvious ones (for example, a
person down on all fours barking like a dog). Consequently, POAL
trainers spend considerable time training employees to see and hear
offers, primarily through "Yes, and" exercises. They begin with
several rounds of the group participants telling a story collectively
[with each person after the opener beginning their line with the
words "Yes, and" (signifying "accept" and "build")]. The trainers
will stop if they hear a negation, an acceptance of an offer without
any building on it, or a multitude of offers. They will invite
discussion on what offers people heard, why they think the scene
was stopped and how they are experiencing this exercise.

Participants are confronted immediately by how much they plan
what they are going to say when it is their turn and by how much
they miss of what has been said. Some say they haven't even been
listening but were "in their heads" while others say they were
evaluating what was said and anticipating – thinking of what they
are going to say that will be funny, make them look good, and the
like. They are struck with how hard this seemingly simple exercise
is. As I understand it, what they are being asked to do is more
than and different from active listening.[4] It is listening *as activity*
(specifically, tool-and-result activity). When participants get the
gist of what is required – listening in order to create the scene (that
is, as a component of making meaning) – their playing "Yes, and"
becomes rigorous practice in getting better at hearing offers and
picking which ones to respond to and how.

The next step in a training workshop is for participants to create
improvisational scenes based on common workplace conversations,
but to apply the principle of "Yes, and" (if not the actual words).
Typically, participants suggest scenes that depict challenging conversations. This exercise takes hearing offers to another level. It is
one thing to accept and build when collectively telling a silly story;
it is quite another to do so in a realistic conversation. Participants
discover that unless they approach the conversation as an improvisational scene that they are actively shaping, they will hear what is
said and respond in pre-determined "scripted" ways that perpetuate the current architecture of conversation and often do not

contribute to building positive relationships between management and staff or between coworkers.

Those participants who are not in any particular scene play an important role. They are instructed to perform as an audience, which allows them to see the people on stage in a new light – as both the characters they are playing and as their work colleagues (managers, peers, supervisees, etc.). Audiences also have eyes and ears that those on stage do not, and they often catch offers that the neophyte improvisers miss. When something obvious such as a boss repeatedly looking at her watch is pointed out, the on-stage improvisers say they did not see it, or they noticed but ignored the offer because they didn't know what to do, given their agenda. This can be an opportunity for them to get better at focusing on the relationship they are creating with the person and not on the outcome they had planned for.

Back at their desks, conference rooms and water coolers, employees try putting "Yes, and" into practice and relating to conversations with coworkers and clients as improvisational scenes. From interviews, supervisory sessions and informal comments after workshops has come a catalogue of the kinds of situations in which they feel this performatory approach is most needed, indicating that they are aware of themselves both as creators of conversations that often turn out to be disappointing or unpleasant, and as performers who can (but might not) perform new conversational scenes. Among the varied conversational snags they report are the following: When . . . I'm assuming I know what's going on; I'm being reactive; someone's blaming; we keep getting stuck in the same scenes; we keep going over and over the past; we're interpreting other people's actions and words instead of being open; we see problems everywhere (Holzman, 2006; interview with Cathy Salit, 12 January 2008).

PLAY AS TRANSFORMATIVE OF THE SOCIO-CULTURAL-EMOTIVE SPACE

In addition to introducing the basic tools of improvisation to businesses and organizations, POAL also brings its signature improvisational exercise of 1-minute "performances of a lifetime." The exercise itself has gone through structural changes over the 10 years since it was introduced. During this time the employment of theatre and improvisational techniques in organizations has expanded dramatically to the point where we can now speak of "theater as intervention" (Nissley, Taylor and Houden, 2004). Moreover, the academic interest in theatre and improvisation with regard to organizations has increased (Montuori, 2003; Nissley, Taylor and Houden, 2004; Nicolaidis and Liotas, 2006; Sawyer, 2000; Weick, 2000). Psychologists and others have turned their attention to adult play, with improvisation being a primary exemplar (Göncü and Perone, 2005; Harris and Daly, no date; Linder, Roos and Victor, 2001). In addition, I have led the performance of a lifetime exercise in the USA and several other countries (in several languages) with a variety of groups, including academics at conferences and other professional gatherings, theatre and psychology students, children, teachers and social service providers. All of these developments have impacted on how I understand this exercise as an activity of working and playing with Vygotsky.

The design of the exercise is simple. Participants come to the stage one at a time to do a 1-minute solo performance that gives expression to something about their life. They are told they can do anything – talk, mime, sing, dance, create a scene, or just stand still and silent. What people do varies in specifics, with the most common scenes taking the form of summaries of life from birth to the present, a typical "day in the life," or an impactful and trans-formative life experience. Immediately following each 1-minute performance, the trainer gives a directorial suggestion to perform a 30-second "sequel" which expands, extends or sheds a different light on what the participant has just performed, and brings another performer or two (who are part of the training team) to the scene to give the participant the added support of a skilled improviser. In the initial setup for the exercise, trainers emphasize the importance of creating a performatory environment that sup-ports everyone to get up on the stage. Typically, they give the audience direction to perform enthusiasm, excitement and loud applause and rehearse a few times. They bring each participant one by one up to the stage with a hearty "Please welcome to the stage, (name)!" Once everyone has performed their 1-minute scene, participants break up into smaller groups for 15–30 minutes to create a short play out of the material they have just performed and seen. They then perform each of their plays for each other. In some trainings, the groups then perform each other's plays. A debrief/discussion period follows.

The workshop in its entirety allows participants opportunities to see, feel and experience being a part of the process of creating with others out of whatever elements there are at their disposal. In this sense, performing on a stage is like looking through a magnifying glass that exposes what our product-socialized eyes cannot normally see – the creative process that goes on all the time in everyday life. Performing their lives and then creating (several times over) something other out of those performances is simultaneously the tool and result of new ways of seeing, feeling and experiencing themselves and each other, as individuals and as the group they are. *Performing themselves is a unique kind of looking at themselves.*

In each component of the performance of a lifetime workshop I see the learning-leading-development aspects of pretend and theatrical play that I introduced in previous chapters when discussing therapy, education and youth development. A dominant feature of the initial 1-minute performances is the collective experience that it *can* be done. In Chapter 3, I referred to the "that-ness" of learning, that component of learning for very young children that is usually lost once they enter school and learning is no longer fused with their everyday relational activities with others. Because, adults support children to do what they do not know how to do, each instance of learning something for children is simultaneously an instance of developing as a learner. I think something like this goes on when adults perform their lives on stage in this exercise. They are being asked to do something they do not know how to do. They are supported to do it by the performatory environment they and the trainers create. In doing the performance, they discover not only how to do what they do not know how to do, but also *that they can do it*. The surprise (often joyous) at showing something of themselves (rather than telling something *about* themselves) in a way they have never done before is palpable. For many participants it is also a break with their usual stories of themselves. As such, it is a new look at who they are.

In the directed 30-second "sequel" both the performer and audience get to see a "story" immediately transform and, perhaps, become aware that the future is created by what is done by themselves and others with what they do, rather than being determined and fixed by what they alone do. The trainer's direction might be a way to highlight the essential playfulness of improv, for example, when the director asks to see a scene in the hospital nursery after a 1-minute performance of giving birth. The meaning of the first scene completely changes through it being built upon and created with. Other times, the trainer's direction is an invitation to the performer to go to a new place, emotionally speaking, for example, when the director asks to see the scene on the golf course between financial advisor and client being interrupted by a phone call telling the financial advisor that his wife has just been in an accident. Again, the first scene is transformed, but this time the performer is challenged to continue the scene having just been thrown off course by unexpected and upsetting news (interview with Cathy Salit, 12 January 2008).[5]

The addition of skilled improvisers to the "sequel" creates another level of zpd, in which the participant can take risks to do even more that she or he does not know how to do. There is now an "other" (or two) to give and receive offers, to build with, and to creatively imitate.

When participants take the individual performances and create different short plays out of them, they are engaging in socially completive activity. They may come away with an awareness that what they have done is beyond what any one of them could do alone and that imagination is not a feature of an internal mind but a collective activity. That three or four groups are doing the same thing and each one has created something completely different reinforces a socialized understanding of the creative process.

Finally, having each group perform each other's improvised plays is another exercise in creative imitation. It is a way to keep building not only on what has been done (the performances that have taken place) but also on who they are (as characters and as an ensemble) and how they perform themselves (as characters and as an ensemble), by incorporating the other.

One other example of this kind of work might emphasize what I see as the developmental value of creative imitation in improvisation. For an international management-consulting firm that wanted help with diversity issues, POAL designed a program that, like the 1-minute performances of a lifetime, gave participants the opportunity to look at themselves as individuals and as a group in a new way. After basic improvisation skill training, the trainers led participants in creating and improvising scenes in which a particular type of person seemed appropriate. For example, a scene set in a baseball locker room would typically call for a group of men. The

POAL trainers, however, set the scene with volunteer participants made up of both men performing as men and women performing as men. Similarly, they created a scene that called for a group of African American women playing cards at a friend's house. Once again, the performers in the scene were African American women performing as African American women, along with white and Asian American men and women performing as African American women. In several scenes like these, identities were mixed up, with people performing as themselves, as one another, and as other types of people different from them.

Upon reflection ("debrief" in consultant lingo) the participants commented that they experienced these performances as being allowed into neighborhoods and homes where they had never been before. According to Salit, who led this exercise,

> What was so fascinating about this work is that it transcended identity politics. We created an environment where identities could be played with and seen as social constructs. The participants perceived each other and themselves in different ways and realized that socially constructed identities can be reconstructed.
>
> (Friedman, 1999, p. 35)

Organizations tend to lock people into roles that diminish creativity and productivity and that can feel bad to be in. The kind of performance work that POAL does gives people an opportunity to engage in creative activity in what Vygotsky called the "imaginative sphere." Improvisation is freedom from "reality's" constraints and as such it provides a playground for adults to try out different ways of being, test the potential of diverse means of sharing, showing and relating, and take a good hard look at themselves. Linder, Roos and Victor (2001) speak to this very point in arguing for the value of play in organizations: "As adults . . . we play the way we are, the way we could, or could not be, and through our engagement in play it shows us what we choose to do, not what we have to do" (Linder, Roos and Victor, 2001, Heading: Transformation, para. 1).

I think of the approach to organizational life that I just described as following a tool-and-result understanding of activity theory, rather than its tool for result version. As I said in Chapter 1, tool-and-result pursues the human capacity to *make new kinds of tools*, while tool for result concentrates on using already existing tools.

POAL and other firms like it, and the organizational studies scholars who write about play and improvisation in organization (whether they are influenced by Vygotsky or not), are interested in relating to and theorizing about the ever-emergent creative capacity of human beings to reshape what exists into something new, to "discover the future that their action creates . . . only as it unfolds" (Barrett, 2006, p. 269). Their orientation is toward the creation rather than the appropriation and replication of culture. In that, they look at the unfolding of the ensemble, self-reflexive and thoroughly subjective (cognitive-emotive) activity of being and becoming.

In contrast, the scholars directly influenced by Vygotsky seem to have chosen to focus on the role of motivation and mediational means in the life of organizations and the people who comprise them. They generally employ a tool for result methodology either to study how organizations and their people use tools to appropriate culture and acquire knowledge or to understand and perhaps change the way knowledge is distributed and tasks are accomplished in organizations.[6] They are interested in the learning organization, and not so much in the playful, improvisational or performatory one. In all of that, they are continuing the tradition of prioritizing cognition as both method and unit of analysis, similar to many activity theorists who study schooling. Like them, they have amassed a solid research agenda and are advancing an important paradigm shift within the field. For one thing, their work draws attention to the language in organizations and draws upon Vygotsky's writings on language, thought and activity to do so. For example, Lissack and Roos (no date) put forth the notion that "languaging" or word choice in usage – as activity – shapes organizations. A shift from a discourse of knowledge in the head to a discourse of knowing as a situated social activity is a shift from a discourse of product and individuals to a discourse of process and social units. Furthermore, Mupepi et al. (2006) posit that a knowledge community's function and success depend largely on its ability to construct a shared mission. Within this, the language used to communicate organizational changes helps shape the experience.

Finally, in urging a postmodern perspective in organizational studies, the social constructionist Kenneth Gergen could well have been describing the socio-cultural activity theory agenda:

> Organizational science may also direct its concerns to the
> dominant and conventional forms of organizations structure

and practice . . . not to extend the modernist quest for the most efficient, productive and profitable . . . rather . . . to inquire into the entity called 'organization' as a form of cultural life.

(Gergen and Thatchenkery, 2006, p. 45)

I suspect that the findings of these kinds of studies of situated learning and distributed cognition in organizations have much to do with the kind of environments workplaces are. Unlike schools, learning is not the mission of organizations and the individual is not the focus of concern. Learning that occurs is not abstracted or isolated from the life of the organization (except possibly during special training courses). The workplace resembles the home environment more than a formal education environment. For preschool children at home, life is not divided into times for play and times for learning; learning is part of whatever the child and others are doing together. For adults in organizations, the work day is not typically divided into times for work and times for learning; the two are integrated and a part of what people are doing.

Even those researchers who limit their study of organizations to how they do learning and knowing would benefit from broadening their conceptions of learning and of social to include the affective. Furthermore, I think that examining play at work would enhance their agenda. Intervention studies, especially, could be enriched by considering how play can transform the social space into a more dynamic adult learning community (Harris and Daley, no date). However, from what I have learned from those who bring play and performance into organizations, I think there is more to recognize and to do. Play creates a "space" to perform imagining, and imagining involves challenging the assumptions of everyday "reality" – this is no small part of what makes it developmental. Improvisational performance is unique as a method for challenging assumptions, because in this kind of play the challenging of assumptions is not a cognitive mental process but a unified cognitive-emotive, mind-body, and socially performed activity. It can be a *stage for development*.

To the extent that business and organizations are structurally and functionally designed to relate to social units (work teams, units, themselves, their industry, their customers, the market, etc.) and not to individuals, they are potentially developmental environments. To the extent that business and organizations need to (or believe they need to) innovate in order to be responsive to rapid and intense changes in the local and global culture, and bring the innovations of play and improvisation performance to the workplace, the people in organizations have opportunities to create developmental stages even as they get the job done.

Chapter 6

Changing relationships

Let us make a special effort to stop communicating with each other, so we can have some conversation.

(Mark Twain)

While I have been a part of the therapeutic, school, outside of school and organizational development projects I have focused on in the preceding chapters, I have done so from my location as director the East Side Institute for Group and Short Term Psychotherapy (Institute). As a research and training center for developing and promoting alternative and radically humanistic approaches to psychology, therapeutics, teaching and learning, the Institute functions as a kind of community think tank. It is both the source of the methodology utilized by the projects I discussed and the beneficiary of the advances their practices make to the ongoing development of the methodology. It is this aspect of our shared history that I have tried to incorporate in telling my stories of social therapy groups, the Barbara Taylor School, and the programs of the All Stars Project and Performance of a Lifetime.

I think of the Institute as a community think tank in other ways as well. For one thing, those who come to train or study with us – either formally in one of our programs or informally through our seminars, independent study or conferences – are a combination of community builders, academics and professionals. What we offer them is what we are learning from our attempt to synthesis innovations from the academic world and from the community. (One of numerous examples is the Institute's 2005 conference on Vygotsky, which brought academic Vygotskians together with both practitioners from community-based programs and curious "ordinary" people; http://www.eastsideinstitute.org/vygoworkplay _workshops.html.)

During the past 10 years, the international reach of the Institute has expanded exponentially, creating an even more heterogeneous mix. Online seminars are open to everyone who wants to participate, regardless of their educational background, and participants range from therapists and educational researchers in Argentina to youth workers in Kenya, from social workers in the USA to community organizers in Taiwan; from applied theatre directors and university theatre professors in South Africa to All Stars volunteers in New York City; from psychologists in Bosnia, Macedonia and Serbia to graduate students from just about anywhere. The International Class, which combines residencies at the Institute with online study and supervision, has trained 50 colleagues, who work in psychology, education, youth development, performance studies and community organizing, from dozens of countries in Africa, Asia, Europe, Central and South America, the USA, Canada and Mexico. Performing the World (PTW) is an international conference, organized by the Institute, that builds community across disciplines and national borders. Since 2001, five gatherings have brought together hundreds of practitioners and scholars, grassroots entrepreneurs and mainstream professionals, who work with performance-based approaches to human development, social transformation and cultural change. In all of these activities the heterogeneity of culture, profession and experience means more material with which to create zpds.

From the Institute's founding in the 1980s, we believed that developing new conceptual frameworks and methodologies required the simultaneous building of a fully participatory community and, further, that these twin tasks required an independent location, that is, one free of institutional ties to university, government, corporation or foundation. The Institute is a small nonprofit organization. Our faculty is all volunteer, and our staff is nearly all volunteer professional and interns. Our modest funding comes from a few hundred individuals. This independent location allows the Institute to be inclusive, to bring together people who do not ordinarily come together, and to do other things that would not be possible in a traditionally funded institution – accept people into our programs without prerequisites or requirements, train nonprofessionals and professionals, collaborate freely and with no strings attached, and act on research and program initiatives with a minimum of bureaucracy. This has been particularly important for psychology and education professionals frustrated by their work in traditional institutions who come to us for a learning experience that is not acquisitional or evaluative, and a community that is not disciplinarily bounded.

From this independent location outside academia proper, Newman and I (and, recently, our younger colleagues) share our scholarship with university-located faculty in the usual ways: writing books and journal articles, presenting at conferences, and dialoguing on list serves. Some academics ignore or discount our work because we are not faculty members of a university department and are not supported by government or foundation grants; to others it makes no difference or is an intriguing plus. Navigating in the often-lofty air of academia has been very challenging for me. Am I an outsider, an insider, both or neither?

I think one's institutional location matters. The Institute's work, conducted outside of academic institutions, speaks directly to academic issues. That in itself, it seems to me, is an issue of academic interest. It raises many questions about disciplinary and institutional boundaries and their impact on the production and dissemination of ideas. Where do they come from and how are they produced? How free is the intellectual marketplace? Does crossing its borders, as the Institute and I do, exacerbate them or begin to dissolve them? The very legitimate academic Kenneth Gergen places the Institute's work as outside what he calls "the tyranny of the normal – the patterns of expectations, obligations and swift sanctions within the core of most disciplines"; it is, to him, a place where it is possible to "risk innovation" (Gergen, 1999, p. 1).

I crisscross the borders because I think there is much more innovation to make possible by people talking to each other across differences in locations and histories. For example, if social therapy groups are effective zones of emotional development, what are the implications for the institution of psychotherapy that the practice has been developed and flourishes outside psychology's physical and methodological borders? Could such a practice, in which people grow emotionally through engaging in the collective activity of breaking down psychology's methodological dualisms, be taught within academia and implemented widely in clinics? Could our work be helpful to those academics and practitioners who are fighting an uphill battle trying to change the medical model of therapeutic treatment? If not, what methodological and political issues does this raise for all of us?

Similarly, if successful approaches to developing children as learners are being implemented outside of schools and independent of university think tanks, what does that say about the current organization of educational research? If performing on stage helps children and youth perform in life, shouldn't educators take a long hard look at their cognitive bias? Could the performatory and improvisational method of the All Stars and the Institute's Developing Teachers Fellowship Program replace the behavior management approach in schools of education? If segregating children into age or "ability" groups is shown to be socially, cognitively and emotionally detrimental, what does school reform mean? And if the All Stars youth programs have effected a unique kind of partnership with business leaders, to support the development of inner-city youth, what are the implications for philanthropy and educational research funding?

Sometimes I raise these kinds of questions directly. At other times, I do not, but they are there under the surface. A few years ago a colleague and I were returning from an international conference where we presented on the same symposium. She told me that many times during the conference she could see the "inside academia/outside academia" tension that the Institute's work generates. As an example, she mentioned how some members of the audience at our symposium seemed to be put off when, during my talk, I gave some facts and figures about the size and scope of the community building projects I am involved in; she thought people took it as self-promoting. She said that this set up an unnecessary barrier – a statement of difference between me and them – that made it difficult for them to hear what in her opinion were sophisticated and important theoretical points that these scholars would be greatly interested in. She wondered if next time I should just omit those details and speak to the theoretical issues.

I recognized what my colleague was talking about, as it happens frequently. I told her I had to speak of my data because they illustrate the very methodology I am putting forth for the audience's consideration. On the one hand, one can see All Stars youth, social therapy clients, trainees and students in training at the Institute, and Fortune 500 executives who learn improv from POAL as analogous to "30 subjects," "two suburban high schools" or "three mother–infant dyads." On the other hand, they are a qualitatively different sort of data set because they are not subjects of an experiment. They are cobuilders of new practices, the tool-and-result of our tool-and-result method. If I left them out and presented only theory, I would be leaving out the environment/activity in and by which the theory was produced. The story I am telling is of bringing Vygotsky from the scientific laboratory to ordinary people and their communities, and what we together have created with him.

My colleague was pointing to the tyranny of the normal, that according to the rules of academic debate, only certain kinds of data produced under certain conditions count as legitimate. I want us to take a look at that, to reflect on our intellectual practice and relational responsibility. Regardless of the specifics of the Institute's work and whether it ultimately makes any contribution to understanding or bettering human life, it presents an opportunity for some healthy self-scrutiny. The issue, as I see it, is not that I am self-promoting and others are not. We all are. It is that we are promoting different ways of seeing and working.

In Chapter 1, I noted two directions of Marx's thinking that influenced Vygotsky – the methodological, which focuses on activity and mind as social, and the analytic-economic, which focuses on the organization of labor. I followed the methodological Marx through Vygotsky to Newman's and my understanding of activity – human beings exercising their power to create and recreate their world, which is inseparable from themselves. Helping people to relate to themselves and each other in this manner entails relating to them as world historic in everyday, mundane matters, that is, as social beings engaged in the life/history-making process of always *becoming*. In this view, instead of being the study of who people *are* and how they got that way, a psychology informed by Marx's method becomes the activity of helping people become who they are not. And the activity of becoming is not the activity of an individual; it is a social, collective and ensemble activity. Vygotsky, following Marx, recognized that if human development was a dialectical, socio-cultural-historical process, then the object of psychology's study was not the intrapsychic state of individuals as they are, but the social activity of producing their becoming.

If there is a synthesis of all that precedes this chapter, I think it is contained in the following conversational exchange posted by a participant in a recent Institute online seminar, entitled "Dialogues on and for Development." The text for the seminar was *Psychological Investigations*, a book of Fred Newman's teaching and supervisory dialogues on social therapy that I put together with my colleague Rafael Mendez (Holzman and Mendez, 2003). About 2 weeks into the 5-week seminar I asked the 25 participants to pick a dialogue and use it as material to create a face-to-face conversation with someone. They would then share online what transpired and we would use that material to continue to create our dialogue. Jim (Papí) asked his 12-year-old daughter Jessie to read one of the dialogues with him because, he told us, "I thought I could have a more performed, less knowing conversation with her than with her Mom or some other adult."[1] The two of them then wrote up their conversation and Jim posted it to the seminar.[2]

> Papí and Jessie are in Jessie's room. Papí has asked Jessie to help him with his homework and Jessie has agreed. They are lying on her bed taking turns reading their parts. Papí helps Jessie with some of the words and they only read the first question and answer in the dialogue. Jessie has read Fred's [Newman] part in the dialogue.
>
> Papí: So what do you think about what you just read?
> Jessie: I think this guy Fred is crazy. Who would want to have therapy part of everyday life? He must have had a lot of problems.
> Papí: Maybe I can read it again to you and maybe you might hear things that you didn't before. (He reads). What do you think now?
> Jessie: I don't think that he is that crazy, maybe therapy could mean other things.
> Papí: Do you still think that therapy everyday is a problem?
> Jessie: Yes.
> Papí: Why?
> Jessie: Because it would be weird to see the same person everyday and they know everything about you.
> Papí: Let me re-read the section where Fred talks about abnormality and how unfortunate it is. (He reads.) So what he is saying here is that therapy doesn't have to be about some person knowing all about you or about some problem that a person has, and maybe it doesn't have to be called therapy.
> Jessie: You mean it could be like working out every day.
> Papí: Yes.

Jessie: Well maybe he (Fred) doesn't have problems. Well maybe he isn't so weird?

Papí: Is that what you think I want to hear? I think you may have a valid point. Maybe Fred is kinda weird. Let me read you this part again about the touching and emotions. (He reads.) How are you thinking about this now that we've read this part again?

Jessie: It would be kinda weird not to have mean people in the world.

Papí: Why?

Jessie: Because, people in this world have someone who is mean to them. They always have an enemy and it would be kinda weird not to, I guess.

Papí: Could I tell you how I understand that?

Jessie: Sure.

Papí: I think that what you are saying is that there is something in what we read [referring to an excerpt from the dialogue] that tells you that if people actually did the things that he is talking about that ____

Jessie: ____ that the whole world would be nicer. *That* would be insane.

The Vygotskian-inspired work I have presented is an attempt to make the world a nicer place – *by engaging people of all ages in making the subjective transformations that I see as required in order to effect revolutionary developmental social change.* I believe that most (and maybe all) people want that but dismiss it as an impossibility. To me this means we have to create opportunities for people to do the impossible. Which means addressing the issue of human development. Which means engaging the conservatism of psychology, both its institutional and folk varieties. Which means being (thought) insane.

In September 1967, 3 years after he received the Nobel Peace Prize and less than a year before he was assassinated, Dr Martin Luther King, Jr delivered a keynote speech to the annual convention of the American Psychological Association in Washington, D.C. His proud confession to being maladjusted speaks to this issue:

You who are in the field of psychology have given us a great word. It is the word maladjusted. It is good certainly [when it implies that] declaring that destructive maladjustment should be destroyed. But on the other hand, I am sure that we will recognize that there are some things in our society, some things in our world, to which we should never be adjusted. There are some things concerning which we must always be maladjusted if we are to be people of good will. We must never adjust ourselves to racial discrimination and racial segregation. We must never adjust ourselves to religious bigotry. We must never adjust ourselves to economic conditions that take necessities from the many to give luxuries to the few. We must never adjust ourselves to the madness of militarism, and the self-defeating effects of physical violence.

Thus, it may well be that our world is in dire need of a new organization, The International Association for the Advancement of Creative Maladjustment. Men and women should be as maladjusted as the prophet Amos, who in the midst of the injustices of his day, could cry out in words that echo across the centuries, "Let justice roll down like waters and righteousness like a mighty stream"; or as maladjusted as Abraham Lincoln, who in the midst of his vacillations finally came to see that this nation could not survive half slave and half free; or as maladjusted as Thomas Jefferson, who in the midst of an age amazingly adjusted to slavery, could scratch across the pages of history, words lifted to cosmic proportions, "We hold these truths to be self evident, that all men are created equal. That they are endowed by their creator with certain inalienable rights. And that among these are life, liberty, and the pursuit of happiness." And through such creative maladjustment, we may be able to emerge from the bleak and desolate midnight of man's inhumanity to man, into the bright and glittering daybreak of freedom and justice.

(King, 1967)

I have additions to Dr King's list of things we should never become adjusted to. First, I would add psychology's basic premises: that the individual is the fundamental unit of human psychological life; that behavior is what is important to study and understand about human beings; that human sociality is an add-on to individuality; and that the emotional and the cognitive are separate realms. Vygotsky tried to develop a psychology without these premises, and his efforts are being continued in significant ways in contemporary socio-cultural activity theory. In addition to psychology's premises, however, there are its institutional biases that it would do well to not become adjusted to: that method is to applied; that explanation, interpretation, categorization and description equal understanding; that objectivity is necessary for scientific discovery; that development is measurable; and that prediction is both possible and desirable. I call these institutional biases because of how deeply rooted they are philosophically and politically in the insistence by psychology that it is a science. Vygotsky's rejection of some of the methodological biases of the psychology of his day was an inspiration to Newman, me and our colleagues to reject those of our day. Rather than accept the natural and physical science paradigm, we have tried to practice psychology *as a cultural-performatory activity* – a participatory process in which people exercise their collective power to create new environments, new social-emotional-intellectual growth, and new forms of social relational life (Newman and Holzman, 1996/2006). Within this framework, the zpd can be considered as a deconstruction–reconstruction of the individuated learning and development model that dominates psychology. In recognizing the relationality and creativity of human life, the zpd avoids psychology's dualisms of individual and society, inner and outer, subjective and objective. These dualisms are embedded in commonly accepted developmental psychology phrases, such as, "children come to know the world," "act upon it" or "construct it" – with child and world thus separated it becomes necessary to come up with explanations for how "in the world" an individual develops. However, if the zpd is the life space in which and how we all live, inseparable from the we who produce it (as Newman and I posit), then explanations for how child and world become "connected" are not needed.

This deconstruction–reconstruction of the individuated learning and development model has political implications as well, for it does not limit us to repeating the past nor to imagining only the possible. The zpd is the socially-historically-culturally produced environment in which and how human beings – determined, to be sure, by sometimes empirically observable circumstances – totally transform these very circumstances, creating something new. The zpd, then, is dialectics in everyday mundane practice, simultaneously the collective producing of development and the environment that makes development possible. The work of the Institute and the programs it has influenced are efforts to create, in all areas of life, continuously overlapping zpds, because in this relational activity forms of life that have become alienated and fossilized are transformed into new forms of life (Newman and Holzman, 1996/2006).

Creating continuously overlapping zpds is a constant running into the folk psychology version of dualistic conceptions of learning and development. To fully accept Vygotsky's claim that people learn and develop socially and his unit of study as social-cultural activity, is to engage the paradoxes it entails: that while life is lived socially it is experienced and related to individualistically; while life is continuous process, it is experienced and related to as space–time products. People live, learn and develop in social units, but are not instructed in ways of creating or functioning effectively in them, or even in how to talk about such things. Conversations are rare among family members on how they want to live together, among students and teachers on how they want to create their classroom, among work groups on how they could function to maximize productivity and creativity, and so on.

Vygotsky's writings have served to inspire and support a paradigm shift in our understanding of human development and learning from ahistorical, acultural, individualistic unfoldings to cultural-historical socially created processes. This new understanding has been a source of inspiration for me and my coworkers and close colleagues to invite children, youth and adults to engage these paradoxes directly and practically – by participating in activities in which discovering how to create a group cannot be avoided (for example, creating the social therapeutic environment, performing school, improvising learning, playing with identity, performing a lifetime). If there is a "classic" tool-and-result activity this is it, for no method exists independent of its unique creation by the group members who are participating and who "discover" their result as their method unfolds.

Socialized to an individuated learning and development model, people enter these therapy groups, classrooms, after school programs and other learning or development environments believing that the way they will learn or get help to change is as individuals. They are given the task of creating a social unit in which they can learn and/or develop, something they not only do not know how to do but think is impossible. They, nevertheless, participate in this collective process. They come face to face with the limitations of trying to learn and grow as individuals as they participate in the process of collective learning and growing. Their new learning and development (a unity of cognition and affect) is both tool and result of the activity of creating the group/ensemble/social unit.

I have come to believe that it is as performers that people are able to engage, in a developmental way, the paradox of experiencing what is a social existence as a separate and individuated one. Children *become*, Vygotsky showed, through their joint performances as other than who they are (speakers, artists, readers, caregivers, and so on). If they were not simultaneously being and becoming, there would be no human civilization. Without any awareness of it, children "create the ensemble" through their relational activity. Their performance as learners leads their development. Once socialized as individuals, this ability to create ensembles for learning-leading-development needs to be rekindled. Conscious performance is a method to do so because it intensifies the relationship between being and becoming. Performance reminds us that we are social beings. Playing with psychological discourse, I characterize the human developmental process as one of creating stages *for* development rather than going through stages *of* development (Holzman, 1997b).

Returning to Jim and 12-year-old Jessie's conversation in the Institute's online seminar, it might seem to be a classic "scaffolding-type" zpd, in which the more capable adult aids the less capable child to go beyond her developmental level and create new learning. I think this way of seeing misses what is most important, from a "developmental/making the world a nicer place" perspective. Jim and Jessie created a new cognitive-affective space, a new form of father–daughter life, a new performance of thought, word and action. Jim found the experience transformative for him, Jessie and their relationship. Here is some of what he wrote to the seminar:

> Here's what was going on, at least what I am aware of. Jessie was annoyed at me when I asked for her help because I had said "no" earlier in the day to her hanging out with friends. She reluctantly said "yes" to helping me. While we were working together one of her friends called and she told the person she was busy helping her dad with his homework. On the first read through Jessie was unenthusiastic about what she had read. I figured that the text was challenging and so I read

it again with some emphasis. I could see that as I re-read different parts that seemed to confuse her and let her tell me about what she thought, that she seemed to be making connections or changing her mind. I tried not to explain too much during my re-reads except to reinforce what she was already saying or clarify vocabulary.

I could see that in just the few minutes that we had spent working together that our relationship had changed and Jessie's attitude had changed and I was also surprised at the leaps she was making in her understanding and the leap she made from a life of therapy every day to a world where everyone was nice. Jessie doesn't allow me to "teach" her and I was really surprised at how quickly she learned what I considered a challenging text and how easy it was for me to simply re-read the text and clarify some of the vocabulary in the course of her helping me with my homework. Usually, she is very resistant to re-reading text on her own or having it read or explained to her.

At dinner with Mom, Jessie brought up the fact that she had helped me with my homework. Later in the conversation she also chimed in when I was telling her mom about an interesting radio program I had been listening to while we were in the car. Jessie usually listens to her ipod and thinks that talk radio is boring. Apparently, she was paying attention and was able to participate in my conversation with Mom in a very thoughtful way. She seemed very proud that she had surprised us with her knowledge.

I felt very well rewarded by my choice and the activity really seemed to shake lose some of the Father–Daughter baggage we've been carrying around and throwing at each other the last few weeks. I am reminded that even when I feel trapped in one of my roles (mean father) there's still (always?) an opportunity to recreate that role/relationship, and it doesn't have to be a big thing that I do, it just has to be something different that we've never done before or that we've done but not become "fossilized" in.

Other seminar participants, too, wrote of conversations they had with family members, friends and colleagues on a chosen dialogue from *Psychological Investigations*. In their write-ups they shared similar experiences as Jim's (for example, "It loosened up our friendship"; "These little moments moved mountains in our every-day conversations"; "I was more self-conscious about performing and creating something together rather than having it all make sense logically – more my usual tendency").

In their article, "Improvisation as adult play," Artin Göncü and Anthony Perone include this comment from Paul Sills, the original director of the Second City improv comedy troupe: "[i]t's not what I know and what you know; it's something that happens between us that's a discovery . . . you can't make this discovery alone. There is always the other" (quoted in Göncü and Perone, 2005, p. 144). We need others to see ourselves. This is as much the case for the institutions of psychology and educational research as it is for fathers and daughters, husbands and wives, CEOs and managers, inner-city youth and Wall Street executives, teachers and students, and therapists and clients. In writing this book I have had to look at these various "ourselves" and "others" from many angles and through different lenses. New ways of seeing, however, emerge through new ways of being. Performing – creating who we are by performing who we are not – is "a new way to be" that does not prioritize thought (or perception) over action, cognition over emotion, or being over becoming. It is activity that is social, communal, reflexive and reconstructive, wherein lies its potential for qualitative socio-cultural transformation.

I and all the people, named and unnamed, in this book have worked and played hard with Vygotsky in the decades since his death. The "problem" of human development and learning is still on the table, even more compelling today because so much is at stake for both the human and physical environment of the planet. But Vygotsky's life and work inspire, and I think that if we continue to work and play together to address the issue of human development – in direct, practical and mundane everyday ways – people might change the world.

Notes

Preface

1 In naming these scholars I do not mean to slight the significant work of Russian scholars or that of colleagues who do not write in English, but only to mention the work with which I am most familiar.

Chapter 1

1 Newman and I have presented our understandings of these constraints and ways to break free of them in a series of books, articles, monographs and chapters since the late 1970s. In particular, the following books contain substantive historical, philosophical and methodological discussions: *Lev Vygotsky: Revolutionary Scientist* (Newman and Holzman, 1993), *Unscientific Psychology: A Cultural-Performatory Approach to Understanding Human Life* (Newman and Holzman, 1996/2006), *The End Of Knowing: A New Developmental Way of Learning* (Newman and Holzman, 1997), *Schools for Growth: Radical Alternatives to Current Educational Models* (Holzman, 1997a), *Performing Psychology: A Postmodern Culture of the Mind* (Holzman, 1999), *Postmodern Psychologies, Societal Practice and Political Life* (Holzman and Morss, 2000), *Psychological Investigations: A Clinician's Guide to Social Therapy* (Holzman and Mendez, 2003), *The Myth of Psychology* (Newman, 1991), *Let's Develop!* (Newman, 1994), and *Performance of a Lifetime* (Newman, 1996). These writings are broadly foundational to many of the ideas put forth in this volume and are cited when reference to a specific publication is warranted.

2 Among the numerous recent critiques of mainstream psychology that include discussions of alternative paradigms and new subject matter for psychology are: Anderson and Gehart (2007); Burman (1994); Cole (1996); Gergen (1994, 1999, 2001); Kvale (1992); McNamee and Gergen (1992; 1999); Morss (1995); Neimeyer and Raskin (2000); Parker (2002); Prilleltensky (1997); Sampson (1993); Shotter (1993a, 1993b); and Soyland (1994).

3 In addition to writing in activity-theoretic and Vygotskian terms, since the late 1970s Newman and I have tried to give expression to our notion of an antiparadigmatic methodology through conceptions from language philosophy combined with Marxist discourse (Newman, 1977/1983, 2000a, 2003; Hood [Holzman] and Newman, 1979; Holzman and Newman, 1985/1988); and postmodern discourse (Newman, 2000b; Newman and Holzman, 1996/2006, 1997, 1999).

4 These topics permeate Vygotsky's writings (and the various translations of them). Rather than citing all the places Vygotsky addressed a particular topic, throughout this volume I have chosen to cite specific writings or to reference particular phrasings when discussing concepts that are not pervasive. The versions of Vygotsky that have been my primary sources and most informed my thinking appear in the following publications: "Thinking and speaking" in *The Collected Works of L. S. Vygotsky, Volume 1* (1987); "The historical meaning of the crisis in psychology" in *The Collected Works of L. S. Vygotsky, Volume 3* (1997a) and *The Essential Vygotsky* (Rieber and Robinson, 2004), and other sections of these volumes; *The Collected Works of L. S. Vygotsky, Volume 2* (1993), *The Collected Works of L. S. Vygotsky, Volume 4* (1997b); and *Mind in Society* (1978).

5 Less widely known are family therapists and counselors who have used Vygotsky's socio-cultural constructed nature of meaning to set forth a dialogic understanding of therapeutic change [for example, Seikkula (1993, 2003) and Strong and Paré, (2004)].

6 The recent development of positive psychology, which focuses on human strengths and virtues rather than pathologies and problems, is concerned with emotions ("positive" ones, such as happiness and optimism). However, it is no less cognitively overdetermined or paradigmatically male than the psychology it purports to replace. It has "changed the subject" but not the adherence to the traditional scientific model (see Selgiman, 2002).

7 In making the distinction between these two methodologies in *Lev Vygotsky: Revolutionary Scientist*, Newman and I speak about kinds of tools:

Even in its simple dictionary denotative use (definition), the term "tool" is exceedingly complex. In contemporary industrial society there are at least two different kinds of tools. There are tools that are mass produced (hammers, screwdrivers, power saws, etc.), and there are tools designed and produced typically by tool-and die-makers, i.e., tools specifically and uniquely designed and developed to assist in the development of other products (including, often, other tools). Because the distinction between these two kinds of tool is of such methodological importance, we want to make clear what it is and what it is not. The distinction we are making is not between mass-produced and hand-produced tools, nor between tools when used for the purpose intended by the maker (hammering a nail with a hammer) and tools when used for another purpose (hitting someone over the head with a hammer), nor between tools that remain unchanged in doing a job and tools that are transformed thereby.

Not everything that is needed or wanted by humankind can be made by simply using (applying) the tools that have already been mass manufactured in modern society. Often we must create a tool which is specifically designed to create what we ultimately wish to produce. The tools of the hardware store and the tools of the tool- and die-maker are qualitatively different in a tool for result/tool-and-result sort of way. Hardware store tools, such as hammers, come to be identified and recognized as usable for a certain end, i.e., they become reified and identified with a certain function and, as such, insofar as the manufactured hammer as a social extension (a tool) of human activity comes to define its human user (as all tool use does), it does so in a predetermining sense.

The toolmaker's tool is different in a most important way. While purposeful, it is not categorically distinguishable from the result achieved by its use. Explicitly created for the purpose of helping to make a specific product, it has no reified prefabricated social identity independent of that activity. Indeed, empirically speaking, such tools are typically no more recognizable as tools than the product (often a quasi-tool or a small part of a larger product) itself is recognizable as product. They are inseparable. It is the productive activity which defines both – the tool *and* the product (the result).

Such tools (or, semantically speaking, such a sense of the word "tool") define their human users quite differently from the way hardware store tools, whether of the physical, symbolic or psychological variety, do. The inner cognitive, attitudinal, creative, linguistic tools developed from the toolmaker type of social tools are incomplete, unapplied, unnamed and, perhaps, unnamable. Expressed more positively, they are inseparable from results in that their essential character (their defining feature) is the activity of their development rather than their function. For their function is inseparable from the activity of their development. They are defined in and by the process of their production.

(Newman and Holzman, 1993, pp. 37–39)

8 Many psychotherapeutic traditions view the practice as an art, among them existential, phenomenological, social constructionist, narrative and some versions of psychoanalysis.

9 On human beings as commodities, Marx had this to say: "Production does not only produce man as a *commodity*, the *human commodity*, man in the form of a *commodity*; in conformity with this situation it produces him as a *mentally* and *physically dehumanized* being" (Marx, 1967, p. 111).

10 Vygotsky's argument against the dominant views of how learning and development are related (the separatist, identity and interactionist

perspectives) is worthy of study. The argument, along with Newman's and my understanding of learning-leading development, is presented in earlier works (Holzman, 1997a; Newman and Holzman, 1993). Here I include an excerpt from those discussions:

> The dialectical unity learning/instruction-leading-development develops as a whole. Learning cannot exist without development and development cannot exist without learning. One is not the cause of the other; rather, they are historical bi-conditions within the ever-changing totality. But, you might be asking, if one is not the cause or precondition of the other, how can Vygotsky say that learning leads development? Doesn't "leads" imply "cause" or at least some "coming before?" What else could he mean when he says that learning is "ahead of" and "in advance of" development?
>
> Herein lies what is most fascinating and revolutionary (and philosophical) about Vygotsky's discovery that learning leads development. For our ordinary language use, which is exceedingly nondialectical, does suggest that "leads" connotes chronology, linearity, hierarchy, or cause, as in "One thing leads to another"; "She led me to the house I was looking for"; "The United States leads the world in . . ."; and "Reading that book led me to pursue a career in astronomy." And indeed, many followers of Vygotsky understand learning-leads-development to mean that learning precedes and/or causes development. In my opinion, such a reading is misguided. For it would simply be the negation of the widely held view that development leads (in linear, chronological, and/or causal fashion) learning, and would thus discount his rejection of the causal-linear model of human development on which both positions are based. Moreover, it denies the totality of Vygotsky's enterprise in which dialectical unity rather than metaphysical duality was central.
>
> (Holzman, 1997a, pp. 58–59)

Chapter 2

1   When asked how this challenge is therapeutic, Newman has said:

> I think it's therapeutic because it helps people to overcome in their own particular way the particular form of their frustration as individuals attempting to grow. It helps people to overcome it because it continually makes the point experientially that it can't be done. It's therapeutic in the way that trying to get someone to throw a ball 400 yards is therapeutic. When it becomes plain that you can't, you then have to consider what you can do, what's do-able, what's possible. It's therapeutic in the way that lots of things in life are therapeutic – they expose the limitations of what you're attempting to do, and if your own limitations are exposed, that's therapeutically helpful as part of the process of coming to more fully appreciate what you can create, what

you can accomplish. And then, if that's accepted and understood collectively, social therapy goes on to teach people how to do new things, which is to grow the group.

(Quoted in Holzman and Mendez, 2003, p. 65)

2 Information about these and related projects is available at their web-sites: East Side Institute: www.eastsideinstitute.org; All Stars Project: www.allstars.org; Performing the World: www.performingtheworld.org; Performance of a Lifetime: www.performanceofalifetime.com.

3 Writing in a different discourse, Cole makes similar points that extend the argument to a methodological critique of standardized testing. He borrows from the work of British psychologist Bartlett on thinking (1958), which distinguished between closed systems (with fixed goals and structures) and two kinds of open systems: experimental thinking (where there is a goal but less structure and fewer constraints) and everyday thinking (which does not obey the constraints of either the closed or experimental system).

> Our conclusion at the end of this work was that by and large, the use of standardized cognitive-psychological experimental procedures implied that a closed analytic system is being successfully imposed upon a more open behavioral system. . . . Insofar as the psychologist's closed system does not capture veridically the elements of the open system it is presumed to model, experimental results systematically misrepresent the life process from which they are derived. The issue of ecological validity then becomes an issue of the violence done to the phenomenon of interest owing to the analytic procedures employed. In this sense, we argued, ecological validity is built directly into the standardized test procedures themselves.
>
> (Cole, 1996, p. 249)

4 Cole has been advocating for scholars to adopt "zo-ped" because, unlike "zpd", it is rich in meaning. First, according to Cole (who has conducted research in Liberia),

> The common name for a shaman in rural Liberia is a *Zo*. [A Zo is] a powerful person who resolves conflicts in the group, who one goes to when ill or in love or angry at someone. In general, people attribute illness to the malevolence of others, so solving medical problems and solving social conflicts are seen as closely related. [Second] *ped* is short for pedagogy. And what does successful, developmentally productive pedagogy require? A little magic and good, theoretically grounded, pedagogical practice.
>
> (Cole, 2008, personal communication)

5 The negative connotation of the word "collective" might also be at play. The Cold War – coupled with social and group psychological theory since Freud and Bion – created wariness and suspicion about collective activity, evoking immediate associations with communism, socialism,

loss of individuality, and the group or mass mind that are still with us, post Cold War.

6 Within the developmental psychology literature, especially of the last two decades, are numerous experimental studies on the imitating capacities of infants (Stern, 2000; Trevarthen, 1998). Many of these studies explore the joint activity/performance/dance between mother and infant, referred to as intersubjectivity. While much of this literature, it should be noted, is framed as providing support for *social cognition*, the emotional bond between mother and infant is often highlighted. This research can be read in the performatory terms that I employ.

7 For example, in "Creativity as a Collective Impulse," Newman comments:

> What guides me, together with the people I'm working with, is a collective creative impulse. In some ways, therapy to me is very much like directing a play. It's not that I don't have some idea of what I'm looking for when I am directing, but what dominates is the creative impulse of the cast, the technicians, and myself as director. By creative impulse, I mean a desire to take what we have collectively – the ideas, the talents, the presuppositions, the tastes, the energies – and to create something new with these inputs, something other than any or all of the inputs. I've come to see the therapeutic work I do as close to the theater work in this sense. I believe that we effect "cure" by creating something new together.
>
> (Newman, quoted in Holzman and Mendez, 2003, p. 74)

8 The term *postmodern therapies* refers to nondiagnostic approaches that focus on the collaborative nature of the conversation and relationship between therapist and client(s). In addition to social therapy, social constructionist, narrative and collaborative therapies are the most well known terms within the postmodern camp. Theoretical discussion and practical examples of these approaches can be found in the following: *Collaborative Therapy* (Anderson and Gehart, 2007); *Maps of Narrative Practice* (White, 2007); *Therapeutic Realities: Collaboration, Oppression and Relational Flow* (Gergen, 2006); *Furthering Talk: Advances in the Discursive Therapies* (Strong and Paré, 2004); *Collaborative Practice in Psychology and Therapy* (Paré and Larner, 2004); *Narrative Therapy in Practice: The Archaeology of Hope* (Monk *et al.*, 1997); and *Therapy as Social Construction* (McNamee and Gergen, 1992).

9 In philosophy one feels forced to look at a concept in a certain way. What I do is suggest, or even invent, other ways of looking at it. I suggest possibilities of which you had not previously thought. You thought that there was one possibility, or only two at most. But I made you think of others. Furthermore, I made you see that it was absurd to expect the concept to conform to those narrow possibilities. Thus your mental cramp is relieved, and you are free to look around the field of use of the expression and to describe the different kinds of uses of it.

> (Wittgenstein, quoted in Monk, 1990, p. 502)

10   I shall in the future again and again draw your attention to what I shall call language-games. These are ways of using signs simpler than those in which we use the signs of our highly complicated everyday language. Language-games are the forms of language with which a child begins to make use of words. The study of language-games is the study of primitive forms of language or primitive languages. If we want to study the problems of truth or falsehood, of the agreement and disagreement of propositions with reality, of the nature of assertion, assumption and question, we shall with great advantage look at primitive forms of language in which these forms of thinking appear without the confusing background of highly complicated processes of thought. When we look at such simple forms of language the mental mist which seems to enshroud our ordinary use of language disappears. We see activities, reactions, which are clear-cut and transparent.

(Wittgenstein, 1965, p. 17)

11   One can also see the cognitive orientation (and lack of reference to emotions and emotional development) in the characterization that Vygotskian scholar Jaan Valsiner gives to psychotherapy. In an essay exploring how research on psychotherapy might be carried out in a way that contributes to new understandings of human development, Valsiner (1995) describes psychotherapy and its process in the following words: "Psychotherapy is a process of goal-oriented transaction that is based on the construction and use of semiotic systems (language use)" (p. 84) and "The processes of psychotherapy can be viewed as a special case of general cultural transmission" (p. 85). A problem-solving approach, no less cognitive, is taken by Lope (1981) in his analysis of the "interactional accomplishment" of a therapeutic zpd. From a different direction, some cognitive therapists upon discovering Vygotsky utilize the concept of the zpd to understand and/or advance their theoretical understanding of their work (for example, Chadwick, 2006).

Chapter 3

1   Among some contemporary Vygotskians who speak and read Russian, there is an ongoing conversation about Vygotsky's use of the Russian word "perezhi'vaniye," which has no exact translation into English. There seems to be agreement that it means something like "experience" and that for Vygotsky, it is a unity of personality and environment. Beyond that, there is lively debate. This is a topic among a select group of scholars (taking place on the Mind, Culture and Activity/xmca listserve) and has not made its way into the more general writings about Vygotsky's work.

2   What I am calling developmental learning stems from my reading of Vygotsky and my experiences as a developmental psychologist, learner, educator and trainer. The methodology of developmental learning emerged from this history. No doubt, some readers will find in my writing resonances with the progressive and free school movements,

other alternative educational movements, or the writings of John Dewey and other seminal philosophers of education.

3 According to the Center on Education Policy, in 2001–2002, the majority of 349 school districts surveyed had increased time spent on English language arts and math in elementary school; 44 per cent had done so by cutting time from other subjects or physical education, recess, and lunch. There is no reason to believe this trend has not continued (McMurrer, 2008). US newspaper and magazine articles decrying school policy toward unstructured and play time in schools are too frequent to document.

4 For some followers of Vygotsky, "leading activity" is an important psychological and pedagogical concept. For example, the Russian psychologists, Davydov and Elkonin, theorize different "leading activities" that correspond to different stages of development: play being the leading activity of early childhood, learning the leading activity of middle childhood, and social relations the leading activity of adolescence (see Davydov, 1988, 1999; Elkonin and Davydov, 1966; Lampert-Shepel, 2003). This approach has gained popularity, particularly the notion of learning activity in middle childhood (see, for example, the more than dozen authors in *Learning Activity and Development*, edited by Hedegaard and Lompscher, 1999).

5 My reading of Vygotsky inspired me to see what I have described and tell the story I tell. A Deweyian, Piagetian, constructivist, and so on, would see something else and tell a different story.

6 Quotes and descriptions of activities from teachers come from a qualitative study conducted by Lobman, discussed in an article, "Improvising with(in) the system: Creating new teacher performances in inner city schools," in press, and from personal communication.

Chapter 4

1 The philosopher Kwame Anthony Appiah has written extensively on identity and cosmopolitanism. He believes that racial identity is a stage in a people's demand to be recognized, but that problems come when identity becomes categorical, defining and rigid. He urges that people engage in "identity play" – a stepping back from our identities to see that they are not always so important and not all of who we are – and move on to postracial identities, which is the "imaginative work of constructing collective identities for a democratic nation in a world of democratic nations" (1996, p. 105).

2 In addition to producing plays, hip-hop cabarets and poetry snaps, Youth OnStage! has a training component, the Youth OnStage! Community Performance School. The school, which is free and runs after school hours and during the summer, is taught by volunteer professionally trained actors, directors and other theater and performing artists. Over 100 young people participate in Youth Onstage!, both in the Community Performance School and in theatre productions as performers, assistant directors, stage managers and production

assistants. Students are recruited from 30 different high schools throughout New York City.

3 The interviews were conducted by Nicole Congrove, a student at NYU's Gallatin School of Individualized Study, who functioned as dramaturg for *Our City*.

4 The quotes from All Stars Project program participants here and in the following pages come from three sources: a video documentary I produced with the Institute in 2002 entitled, "Young People Learn by Studying Themselves"; and a focus group and a survey conducted by the All Stars Project in 2008. The latter material is quoted with permission from the All Stars.

5 The All Stars Talent Show Network involves young people from the five boroughs of New York City and poor communities throughout Newark, NJ; San Francisco and Oakland, CA; and Chicago, IL. The All Stars Talent Show Network is also produced by local organizations in Atlanta, Boston, Los Angeles, and internationally in Amsterdam, the Netherlands.

6 The Development School for Youth recruits students from 60 high schools in the five boroughs of New York City and in schools in Newark, NJ. In 2007, there were 178 graduates from the DSY, and over 50 corporations that sponsored paid summer internships for them.

7 The early All Stars outreach/fundraising (conducted on street corners and at the doors of people's homes) was not so much a partnership as it was broad support from all kinds of people for the ASTSN. According to Kurlander, when the All Stars began to receive larger gifts from business people it raised the question of how to keep these people engaged and the possibility of building something new with the business community. In the decade+ since the DSY was founded, the All Stars has continued to develop its unique model of philanthropy. Commenting further, Kurlander states:

> We are raising private money in a traditionally public sector domain, namely anti-poverty and youth development work. Our private funding is key to how our programs have become engines for innovation. Government programs are constrained, politicized and largely ineffective. Our privately funded programs serve as laboratories for innovative approaches.
>
> (Kurlander, 2008, personal communication)

Chapter 5

1 Among the hundreds of book and speech titles competing for the business leadership eyes and ears are the following: *Strategic Thinking and the New Science: Planning in the Midst of Chaos*; *Complexity and Change*; *The Complexity Advantage: How the Science of Complexity Can Help Your Business Achieve Peak Performance*; *Peak Performance: Aligning the Hearts and Minds of Your Employees*; *The Passionate Organization: Igniting the Fire of Employee Commitment*; *Collaborative*

Creativity: Unleashing the Power of Shared Thinking; Building Team Power: How to Unleash the Collaborative Genius of Work Teams; Igniting Innovation – Inspiring Organizations by Managing Creativity; Creativity and the Management of Change; Meeting the Art of Creative Collaboration; Corporate Creativity; The Creative Executive: How Business Leaders Innovate by Stimulating Passion, Intuition and Creativity.

2 For example, the major graduate schools of business offer courses that apply complexity and chaos theory to organizations, look at organizations as enacted systems, and teach methods to foster and manage innovation and use improvisation in business.

3 POAL's global client list includes PricewaterhouseCoopers, Arcelor-Mittal, Barclays Bank, Citigroup, Booz Allen Hamilton, Infosys, Lehman Brothers, and the United States Olympic Committee. In addition to its full time staff, over 30 trainers, actors, directors, coaches and playwrights work with POAL on a freelance basis.

4 Active listening in conflict resolution refers to techniques for listening and responding that focus the attention fully on the speaker. The listener is trained to attend to the speaker and repeat in the listener's own words what he or she thinks the speaker has said. (Conflict Research Consortium, University of Colorado, USA, http://www.colorado.edu/conflict/peace/treatment/activel.htm, accessed 20 February, 2008.) The term is used more generally, but with the same intent, in counseling, human resource and social work training contexts.

5 POAL's website (www.performanceofalifetime.com) contains additional vignettes as part of client stories.

6 The work of Yrjö Engeström and the Center for Activity Theory and Developmental Work Research in Helsinki works with somewhat different aspects of Vygotsky's work to study transformations in work and organizations. Engeström's work combines micro level analysis of discourse and interaction, with historical analysis and modeling of organizations as activity systems working through developmental contradictions (see Engeström, 2005; Engeström, Engeström and Kerosuo, 2003; and Engeström and Kerosuo, 2007).

Chapter 6

1 Jim's write up of the conversation and his reflections on it are included here with permission from him and his daughter, Jessie.

2 Jim and Jessie were reading the following excerpt from Dialogue 17: Improvisational Learning (Holzman and Mendez, 2003, pp. 86–87):

Therapist-in-training 1: I'm not sure how to ask this question or if it is a question – what are your thoughts, comments, reactions, etc., on improvisation, therapy, and life?

Fred: I now think that life is much more improvisational than I once thought. I think improvisation is something we can learn and that it helps us live our lives better. My picture of the culture in which we live is that it tends to be very role over-determined. I don't mean that as a moral critique. We teach people to be who they are, to adjust to society, by putting them in roles – and we do this in a way that we think is positive. We try to help them see their roles. That can be of value; I think it is important, in some sense, to learn who we are. On the other hand, so much of life is lived between the cracks, in the subjective nuances of how we deal with each other.

As for therapeutics, I think it's too bad that psychotherapy has been so associated with abnormality. That this is changing is a very good thing. Emotional/developmental skills are an important part of what we need to learn everywhere – in schools and families and so on. Maybe we are heading towards a time where therapy is part of life and maybe it will not be called therapy.

People can become very much better at emotional interaction; it is something you can learn. There is still a tendency to believe that normal emotionality is simply picked up automatically. I don't agree. I think it is unfortunate that we don't learn how to touch each other, how to relate to each other, how to be with each other, how to give, how to create social environments. Will the day come? It probably will not happen in my lifetime or in most of our lifetimes.

Therapist-in-training 1: I'm not sure what you mean by improvisation. Fred: For me improvisation is the skill of creating something unexpected, outside of the boundaries of role-governed activity. You've seen those puzzles in which you are supposed to connect the dots and the only way you can do that is to go outside an imposed box? I think that improvisation is going outside of the socially imposed boxes that we all live our lives in.

Sometimes there is nothing better than being in a role; I don't think that people should improvise when they are crossing the streets in New York City. There I support role-governed, rule-governed behavior 100 percent. On the other hand, there are so many life situations in which it would be wonderful and developmental to be able to not be constrained by that, for example, when relating to a loved one to be able to continue to grow the relationship, to consciously try new things, even at the dinner table. Even if we choose not to do something different, it would be nice to have that option. We can be a very conservative, over-determined species, but we also have the capacity for choosing to step out of the box.

References

Allal, L., and Pelgrims, A. (2000). Assessment of or in the zone of proximal development. *Learning and Instruction, 10*(2), 137–152.

American Psychiatric Association (2000). *Diagnostic and statistical manual of mental disorders DSM-IV-TR, Fourth Edition.* Washington, DC: APA.

American Psychological Association Policy and Planning Board (2005). APA 2020: A perfect vision for psychology; 2004 five-year report of the Policy and Planning Board. *American Psychologist, 60,* 512–522.

Anderson, H. (1997). *Conversation, language and possibilities: A postmodern approach to therapy.* New York: Basic Books.

Anderson, H., and Gehart, D. (2007). (Eds.). *Collaborative therapy: Relationships and conversations that make a difference.* New York: Routledge.

Appiah, K. A. (1996). Race, culture, identity: Misunderstood connections. In K. A. Appiah and A. Gutmann (Eds.), *Color consciousness: The political morality of race* (pp. 30–105). Princeton, NJ: Princeton University Press.

Arts Education Partnership (1999). *Champions of change: The impact of the arts on learning.* Washington, DC: Arts Education Partnership.

ASCD Smart Brief (January, 2008). Available at http://www.smartbrief. com/.

Baker, G. P. (1992). Some remarks on "language" and "grammar." *Grazer Philosophische Studien, 42,* 107–131.

Baker-Sennett, J., and Matusov, E. (1997). School "performance": Improvisational processes in development and education. In R. K. Sawyer (Ed.), *Creativity in performance* (pp. 197–212). New York: Ablex.

Barrett, F. (2006). Living in organizations: Lessons from jazz improvisation. In S. McNamee and D. M. Hosking (Eds.), *The social construction of organization* (pp. 269–277). Denmark: Liber and Copenhagen Business School Press.

Bartlett, F. (1958). *Thinking*. New York: Basic Books.

Barton, W. H., Watkins, M., and Jarjoura, R. (1997). Youths and communities: Toward comprehensive strategies for youth development. *Social Work*, *42*, 483–494.

Bateson, G. (1972). Social planning and the concept of deutero-learning. In G. Bateson, *Steps to an ecology of mind* (pp. 159–176). New York: Ballantine. Originally published as Bateson, G. (1942). Comment on "The comparative study of culture and the purposive cultivation of democratic values" by Margaret Mead. In L. Bryson and L. Finkelstein (Eds.), *Science, philosophy and religion: second symposium* (pp. 81–97). New York: Conference on Science, Philosophy and Religion in Their Relation to the Democratic Way of Life, Inc.

Berk, L. E., and Winsler, A. (1995). *Scaffolding children's learning: Vygotsky and early childhood education*. Washington, DC: National Association for the Education of Young Children.

Betts, J. D. (2006). Multimedia arts learning in an activity system: New literacies for at-risk children. *International Journal of Education & the Arts*, *7*, 7. From http://www.ijea.org/v7n7/index, accessed 8 August 2008.

Blantern, J., and Anderson-Wallace, M. (2006). Patterns of engagement. In D. M. Hosking and S. McNamee (Eds.), *The social construction of organization* (pp. 70–85). Denmark: Liber and Copenhagen Business School Press.

Blatner, A. (1997). *The art of play*. New York: Brunner/Mazel.

Bodilly, S., and Beckett, M. K. (2005). *Making out of school time matter: Evidence for an action agenda*. San Francisco, CA: Rand.

Borko, H., and Livingston, C. (1989). Cognition and improvisation: Differences in mathematics instruction by expert and novice teachers. *American Educational Research Journal*, *26*, 473–498.

Bridglall, B. L. (2005). Varieties of supplementary education interventions. In E. W. Gordon, B. L. Bridglall, and A. S. Meroe (Eds.), *Supplementary education: The hidden curriculum of high academic achievement* (pp. 190–210). Latham, MD: Rowman and Littlefield.

Brown, K., and Cole, M. (no date). Cultural historical activity theory and the expansion of opportunities for learning after school. From http://lchc.ucsd.edu/People/MCole/browncole.html, accessed 13 June 2006.

Bruner, J. (1996). Celebrating divergence: Piaget and Vygotsky. Keynote Address, Growing Mind Conference, Geneva, September 1996.

Bruner, J. (2004). Introduction to *Thinking and speech*. In R. W. Reiber and D. K. Robinson (Eds.), *The essential Vygotsky* (pp. 9–25). New York: Kluwer Academic/Plenum.

Burman, E. (1994). *Deconstructing developmental psychology*. London: Routledge.

Carnegie Council on Adolescent Development (1992). *A matter of time:*

Risk and opportunity in the nonschool hours. Carnegie Council Monograph. Available at http://www.carnegie.org/ccadpubs.htm, accessed 1 December 2007.

Chadwick, P. (2006). *Person-centered cognitive therapy for distressing psychosis.* Chichester, UK: Wiley.

Childress, H. (1998). Seventeen reasons why football is better than high school. *Phi Delta Kappan, 79,* 616–620.

Cole, M. (1996). *Cultural psychology: A once and future discipline.* Cambridge, MA: Harvard University Press.

Cole, M., and the Distributed Literacy Consortium (2006). *The fifth dimension: An after-school program built on diversity.* New York: Russell Sage Foundation.

Cole, M., Hood [Holzman], L., and McDermott, R. P. (1978). *Ecological niche-picking: Ecological invalidity as an axiom of experimental cognitive psychology.* New York: Rockefeller University, Laboratory of Comparative Human Cognition.

Cooper, C. (2004) "A struggle well worth having": The uses of theatre-in-education (TIE) for learning. *Support for Learning, 19*(2), 81–87. DOI:10.1111/j.0268-2141.2004.00325.x

Csíkszentmihályi, M. (1991). *Flow: The psychology of optimal experience.* New York: HarperCollins.

Danziger, K. (1997). *Naming the mind: How psychology found its language.* London: Sage.

Davydov, V. V. (1988). Problems of developmental teaching. *Soviet Education, 30*(8), 15–97.

Davydov, V. V. (1999). What is real learning activity? In M. Hedegaard and J. Lompscher (Eds.), *Learning activity and development* (pp. 123–138). Aarhus, Denmark: Aarhus University Press.

DiPardo, A., and Schnack, P. (2004). Expanding the web of meaning: Thought and emotion in an intergenerational reading and writing program. *Reading Research Quarterly, 39,* 14–37.

Drucker, P. F. (1988). The coming of the new organization. *Harvard Business Review, 66*(1), 45–53.

Elkonin, D. B., and Davydov, V. V. (1966). *Learning possibilities at different ages.* Moscow: Prosvescenie.

Engeström, Y. (2005). *Developmental work research: Expanding activity theory in practice.* Berlin: Lehmanns Media.

Engeström, Y., and Kerosuo, H. (2007). From workplace learning to interorganizational learning and back: The contribution of activity theory. *Journal of Workplace Learning, 19,* 336–342.

Engeström, Y., Engeström, R., and Kerosuo, H. (2003). The discursive construction of collaborative care. *Applied Linguistics, Special Issue, 24,* 286–315.

Epstein, R. (2007). Why high schools must go: An interview with Leon Botstein. *Phi Delta Kappan*, *88*, 659–663.

Feldman, N. (in press). Assisting children in the creation of new life performances: Expanding possibilities for social and emotional development. *Child and Adolescent Social Work Journal*.

Finn, J. L., and Checkoway, B. (1995). Young people as competent community builders: A challenge to social work. *Social Work*, *43*, 335–345.

Friedman, D. (1990). The Soviet Union in the 1920s – An historical laboratory. *Practice: The Magazine of Psychology and Political Economy*, *7*(3), 4–9.

Friedman, D. (1999). Performance of a Lifetime: Interactive growth theatre and the development of performance in everyday life. *Theatre Insight*, *10*(2), 25–38.

Friedman, D. (2003). Extra theatrical performance: Acting leaves home and finds a whole new world. *Backstage*, August 1, 24–27.

Fulani, L. (2004). Résumé stories. In H. L. Gates, Jr (Ed.), *America behind the color line: Dialogues with African Americans* (pp. 104–121). New York: Warner Books.

Gajdamaschko, N. (2005). Vygotsky on imagination: Why an understanding of the imagination is an important issue for schoolteachers. *Teaching Education*, *16*, 13–22.

Gates, H. L. Jr. (2004). (Ed.). *America behind the color line: Dialogues with African Americans*. New York: Warner Books.

Gergen, K. J. (1991). *The saturated self: Dilemmas of identity in contemporary life*. New York: Basic Books.

Gergen, K. J. (1994). *Realities and relationships: Soundings in social construction*. Cambridge, MA: Harvard University Press.

Gergen, K. J. (1999). Foreward. In L. Holzman (Ed.), *Performing psychology: A postmodern culture of the mind* (pp. 1–2). New York: Routledge.

Gergen, K. J. (2001). *Social construction in context*. London: Sage.

Gergen, K. J. (2006). *Therapeutic realities: Collaboration, oppression and relational flow*. Chagrin Falls, OH: Taos Institute Publications.

Gergen, K. J., and Thatchenkery, T. (2006). Organizational science and the promise of postmodernism. In S. McNamee and D. M. Hosking (Eds.), *The social construction of organization* (pp. 34–51). Denmark: Liber and Copenhagen Business School Press.

Glick, J. (2004). The history of the development of higher mental function. In R. W. Rieber and D. K. Robinson (Eds.), *The essential Vygotsky* (pp. 345–357). New York: Kluwer Academic/Plenum.

Goldstein, L. S. (1999). The relational zone: The role of caring relationships in the co-construction of mind. *American Educational Research Journal*, *36*, 647–673.

Göncü, A., and Gaskins, S. (2007). (Eds.). *Play and development:*

Evolutionary, sociocultural and functional perspectives. New York: Psychology Press.

Göncü, A., and Perone, A. (2005). Pretend play as a life-span activity. *Topoi, 24,* 137–147.

Gordon, E. W. (1999). *Education and justice: A view from the back of the bus.* New York: Teachers College Press.

Gordon, E. W., Bridglall, B. L., and Meroe, A. S. (2005). *Supplementary education: The hidden curriculum of high academic achievement.* Latham, MD: Rowman and Littlefield.

Griggs, T. (2001). Teaching as acting: Considering acting as epistemology and its use in teaching and teacher preparation. *Teacher Education Quarterly, 28*(2), 23–37.

Haggbloom, S. J., Warnick, R., Warnick, J. E., Jones, V. K., Yarbrough, G. L., Russell, T. M., *et al.* (2002). The 100 most eminent psychologists of the twentieth century. *Review of General Psychology, 6,* 139–152.

Harris, P., and Daley, J. (no date). Social capital and adult learning: Exploring play in institutional settings. From http://www.ala.asn.au/conf/2006/papers/refereed%20papers/ALA2006_Paper_%20Harris Daley_S20_.pdf, accessed 1 December 2007.

Heath, S. B. (2000). Making learning work. *Afterschool Matters: Dialogues in Philosophy, Practice and Evaluation, 1,* 33–45.

Heath, S. B., Soep, E., and Roach, A. (1998). Living the arts through language and learning: A report on community-based youth organizations. *Americans for the Arts Monographs, 2*(7), 1–20.

Hedegaard, M., and Lompscher, J. (1999). *Learning activity and development.* Aarhus, Denmark: Aarhus University Press.

Henig, R. M. (2004). Sorry. Your eating disorder doesn't meet our criteria. *New York Times,* 30 November 2004. Available at http://www.nytimes.com/2004/11/30/health/psychology/30eat.html?pagewanted=2&_r=1&sq=eating%20disorders&st=cse&oref=slogin&scp=8.

Holzman, L. (1990). Lev and let Lev: An interview on the life and works of Lev Vygotsky. *Practice: The Magazine of Psychology and Political Economy, 7*(3), 11–23.

Holzman, L. (1993). The Rainbow Curriculum in democracy-centered schools: A new approach to helping children learn. *Inquiry: Critical Thinking Across the Disciplines, 11*(3), 3–5.

Holzman, L. (1995). Creating developmental learning environments: A Vygotskian practice. *School Psychology International, 16,* 199–212.

Holzman, L. (1997a). *Schools for growth: Radical alternatives to current educational models.* Mahwah, NJ: Lawrence Erlbaum Associates.

Holzman, L. (1997b). The developmental stage. *Special Children,* June/July, 32–35.

Holzman, L. (1999). (Ed.), *Performing psychology: A postmodern culture of the mind.* New York: Routledge.

Holzman, L. (2000). Performative psychology: An untapped resource for educators. *Educational and Child Psychology*, *17*(3), 86–103.

Holzman, L. (2002). *Young people learn by studying themselves: The All Stars Talent Show in action*. New York: East Side Institute for Short Term Psychotherapy.

Holzman, L. (2006). Lev Vygotsky and the new performative psychology: Implications for business and organizations. In D. M. Hosking and S. McNamee (Eds.), *The social construction of organization* (pp. 254–268). Denmark: Liber and Copenhagen Business School Press.

Holzman, L. and Mendez, R. (2003). *Psychological investigations: A clinician's guide to social therapy*. New York: Brunner-Routledge.

Holzman, L., and Morss, J. (Eds.) (2000). *Postmodern psychologies, societal practice and political life*. New York: Routledge.

Holzman, L., and Newman, F. (1985/1988). History as an anti-paradigm. *Practice: The Journal of Politics, Economics, Psychology, Sociology & Culture*, *3*, 3. Reprinted in L. Holzman and H. Polk (Eds.), *History is the cure: A social therapy reader* (pp. 55–67). New York: Practice Press.

Holzman, L., and Newman, F. (1987). Language and thought about history. In M. Hickmann (Ed.), *Social and functional approaches to language and thought* (pp. 109–121). London: Academic Press.

Holzman, L., and Newman, F., with T. Strong (2004). Power, authority and pointless activity: The developmental discourse of social therapy. In T. Strong and D. Paré (Eds.), *Furthering talk: Advances in discursive therapies* (pp. 73–86). New York: Kluwer Academic.

Hood [Holzman], L., and Newman, F. (1979). *The practice of method: An introduction to the foundations of social therapy*. New York: New York Institute.

Hood [Holzman], L., McDermott, R. P., and Cole, M. (1980). "Let's try to make it a good day" – Some not so simple ways. *Discourse Processes*, *3*, 155–168.

Hood [Holzman], L., Fiess, K., and Aron, J. (1982). Growing up explained: Vygotskians look at the language of causality. In C. Brainerd and M. Pressley (Eds.), *Verbal processes in children* (pp. 265–286). New York: Springer-Verlag.

John-Steiner, V., and Souberman, E. (1978). Afterword. In L. S. Vygotsky, *Mind in society* (pp. 121–133). Cambridge, MA: Harvard University Press.

Johnstone, K. (1981). *Improv: Improvisation and the theatre*. New York: Routledge.

Jones, J. C. (2003). Transforming school culture through the arts. *The Evaluation Exchange*, *IX*(4), Winter 2003/2004, p. 18.

Kane, P. (1995). *The play ethic*. New York: Macmillan.

King, M. L. Jr (1967). The role of the behavioral scientist in the civil rights movement. *APA Monitor Online*. From http://www.apa.org/monitor/jan99/king.html, accessed 10 September 2007.

Klein, J. (2007). Teaching theater today. *Theater Topics*, *17*(2), 169–170.

Kozol, J. (2005). *The shame of the nation: The restoration of apartheid schooling in America*. New York: Crown.

Kuhn, T. S. (1962). *The structure of scientific revolutions*. Chicago, IL: University of Chicago Press.

Kvale, S. (1992). (Ed.), *Psychology and postmodernism*. London: Sage.

LaCerva, C. (1992). Talking about talking about sex: The organization of possibilities. In J. T. Sears (Ed.), *Sexuality and the curriculum: The politics and practice of sexuality education* (pp. 124–137). New York: Teachers College Press.

Lampert-Shepel, E. (September–October, 2003). (Ed.) Learning activity. *Journal of Russian and East European Psychology*, *41*(4).

Lantoff, J. P. (Ed.). (2000). *Sociocultural theory and second language learning*. Oxford: Oxford University Press.

Levitan, K. (1982). *One is not born a personality: Profiles of Soviet education psychologists*. Moscow: Progress Publishers.

Lidz, C. S., and Gindis, B. (2003). Dynamic assessment of the evolving cognitive functions in children. In A. Kozulin, B. Gindis, V. S. Ageyev, and S. M. Miller (Eds.), *Vygotsky's educational theory in cultural context* (pp. 99–116). New York: Cambridge University Press.

Linder, M.-O., Roos, J., and Victor, B. (2001). Play in organizations. Working Paper 2, Imagination Lab. From http://www.imagilab.org/pdf/wp01/WP2.pdf, accessed 12 December 2007.

Lissack, M., and Roos, J. (no date). Words count: Viewing organizations as emerging systems of languaging. From http://lissack.com/writings/AMRfinal.pdf, accessed 10 January 2008.

Lobman, C. (2003). What should we create today? Improvisational teaching in early childhood classrooms. *International Journal for Early Years Education*, *23*, 133–145.

Lobman, C. (2005). "Yes and." The uses of improvisation for early childhood teacher development. *The Journal of Early Childhood Teacher Education*, *26*, 315–319.

Lobman, C. (in press). Improvising with(in) the system: Creating new teacher performances in inner city schools. In R. K. Sawyer (Ed.), *The teaching paradox: Creative improvisation in the classroom*. Cambridge: Cambridge University Press.

Lobman, C. (under review). Improvisation: A postmodern playground for early childhood teachers. Submitted for publication to S. Ryan and S. Grieshaber (Eds.), *Putting postmodern theories into practice*. New York: JAI Press.

Lobman, C., and Lundquist, M. (2007). *Unscripted learning: Using improv activities across the K-8 curriculum*. New York: Teachers College Press.

Lope, L. (1981). Problem solving in a human relationship: The inter-actional accomplishment of a "Zone of Proximal Development" in therapy. *The Quarterly Newsletter of the Laboratory of Comparative Human Cognition, 3*(1), 1–5.

McDermott, R. P., and Hood [Holzman], L. (1982). Institutional psy-chology and the ethnography of schooling. In P. Gilmore and A. Glatthorn (Eds.), *Children in and out of school: Ethnography and edu-cation* (pp. 232–249). Washington, DC: Center for Applied Linguistics.

McLeod, J. (1997). *Narrative and psychotherapy.* London: Sage.

McMurrer, J. (2008). Instructional time in elementary schools: A closer look at changes in specific subjects. Center on Educational Policy. From http://www.cep-dc.org/_data/n_0001/resources/live/InstructionalTime Feb2008.pdf, accessed 3 February 2008.

McNamee, S., and Gergen, K. J. (Eds.), (1992). *Therapy as social construction.* London: Sage.

McNamee, S., and Gergen, K. J. (1999). *Relational responsibility: Resources for sustainable dialogue.* Thousand Oaks, CA: Sage.

MacNaughton, G., and Williams, G. (1998). *Techniques for teaching young children: Choices in theory and practice.* French Forests, Australia: Longman.

Mahoney, J. L., Larson, R. W., and Eccles, J. S. (2005). (Eds.). *Organized activities as contexts of development: Extracurricular activities, after school and community programs.* Mahwah, NJ: Lawrence Erlbaum Associates.

Marx, K. (1967). Economic and philosophical manuscripts. In E. Fromm (Ed.), *Marx's concept of man* (pp. 90–196). New York: Frederick Ungar.

Marx, K. (1974). Theses on Feuerbach. In K. Marx and F. Engels, *The German Ideology* (pp. 121–123). New York: International Publishers.

Miller, J. B. (1976). *Toward a new psychology of women.* Boston, MA: Beacon.

Monk, G., Winslade, J., Crocket, K., and Epston, D. (Eds.) (1997). *Narrative therapy in practice: The archaeology of hope.* San Francisco, CA: Jossey-Bass.

Monk, R. (1990). *Ludwig Wittgenstein: The duty of genius.* New York: Penguin.

Montuori, A. (2003). The complexity of improvisation and the improvisa-tion of complexity: Social science, art and creativity. *Human Relations, 56,* 237–255. Also from http://hum.sagepub.com.ogi/content/abstract/ 56/2/237, accessed 12 November 2007.

Morss, J. (1995). *Growing critical: Alternatives to developmental psychology.* London: Routledge.

Mupepi, S. C., Mupepi, M. G., Tenkasi, R., and Sorensen, P. (2006). Changing the mindset: Transforming organizations into high energized

and performance organization. From http://www.midwestacademy.org/
Proceedings/2006/papers/paper17.pdf, accessed 10 December 2007.

Nachmanovitch, S. (1990). *Free play: Improvisation in life and art*. New
York: Putnam.

National Collaboration for Youth (1996). *Position statement on accountability and evaluation in youth development organizations*. Washington,
DC: National Collaboration for Youth.

Neimeyer, R. A., and Raskin, J. D. (2000). Varieties of constructivism in
psychotherapy. In K. Dobson (Ed.), *Handbook of cognitive behavioral
therapies* (2nd ed., pp. 393–430). New York: Guilford.

Nelmes, P. (2000). Developing a conceptual framework for the role of the
emotions in the language of teaching and learning. Thematic Group 2,
European Research in Mathematics Education III. From http://www.
dm.unipi.it/vdidattica/CERME3/proceedings/tableofcontents_cerme3.
html, accessed 1 December 2007.

Newman, D., Griffin, P., and Cole, M. (1989). *The construction zone:
Working for cognitive change in school*. Cambridge: Cambridge
University Press.

Newman, F. (1977/1983). Practical-critical activities: Toward a non-
paradigmist analysis of contemporary US social deterioration.
Reprinted in *Practice: The Journal of Politics, Economics, Psychology,
Sociology & Culture, 1*(2), 20–28.

Newman, F. (1991). *The myth of psychology*. New York: Castillo
International.

Newman, F. (1994). *Let's develop! A guide to continuous personal growth*.
New York: Castillo International.

Newman, F. (1996). *Performance of a lifetime: A practical-philosophical
guide to the joyous life*. New York: Castillo International.

Newman, F. (1999). A therapeutic deconstruction of the illusion of self. In
L. Holzman (Ed.), *Performing psychology: A postmodern culture of the
mind* (pp. 111–132). New York: Routledge.

Newman, F. (2000a). The performance of revolution (more thoughts on
the postmodernization of Marxism). In L. Holzman and J. Morss
(Eds.), *Postmodern psychologies, societal practice and political life* (pp.
165–176). New York: Routledge.

Newman, F. (2000b). Does a story need a theory? Understanding the
methodology of narrative therapy. In D. Fee (Ed.), *Pathology and the
postmodern: Mental illness as discourse and experience* (pp. 248–262).
London: Sage.

Newman, F. (2003). Undecidable emotions (What is social therapy? And
how is it revolutionary?). *Journal of Constructivist Psychology, 16*, 215–
232.

Newman, F., and Holzman, L. (1993). *Lev Vygotsky: Revolutionary
scientist*. London: Routledge.

— Newman, F., and Holzman, L. (1996/2006). *Unscientific psychology: A cultural-performatory approach to understanding human life.* Lincoln, NE: iUniverse Inc. (originally published Westport CT: Praeger).

Newman, F., and Holzman, L. (1997). *The end of knowing: A new developmental way of learning.* London: Routledge.

Newman, F., and Holzman, L. (1999). Beyond narrative to performed conversation ('In the beginning' comes much later). *Journal of Constructivist Psychology, 12,* 23–40.

Nicolaidis, C., and Liotas, N. (2006). A role for theatre in the education, training and thinking processes of managers. *Industry and Higher Education, 20,* 19–24.

Nicolopoulou, A., and Cole, M. (1993). The generation and transmission of shared knowledge in the culture of collaborative learning: The Fifth Dimension, its play world, and its institutional contexts. In E. A. Forman, N. Minick, and C. A. Stone (Eds.), *Contexts for learning: sociocultural dynamics in children's development* (pp. 283–314). New York: Oxford University Press.

Nissley, N., Taylor, S., and Houden, L. (2004). The politics of performance in organization theatre-based training and intervention. *Organizational Studies, 25*(5), 817–839.

No Child Left Behind Act of 2001, Pub.L.No.107-110 (2001).

Noddings, N. (1984). *Caring.* Berkeley, CA: University of California Press.

Paré, D. A., and Larner, G. (2004). (Eds.), *Collaborative practice in psychology and therapy.* New York: Haworth Clinical Practice Press.

Parker, I. (2002). *Critical discursive psychology.* New York: Palgrave Macmillan.

Penuel, W. (1998). Adult guidance in youth development revisited: Identity construction in youth organizations. From http://psych.hanover.edu/vygotsky/penuel.html, accessed 30 January 2008.

Pineau, E. L. (1994). Teaching is performance: Reconceptualizing a problematic metaphor. *American Educational Research Journal, 31*(1), 3–25.

Pittman, K., and Cahill, M. (1991). A new vision: Promoting youth development (Commissioned Paper No. 3). Washington, DC: Academy for Educational Development, Center for Youth Development and Policy Research.

Portes, P. R. (2005, and under review). Cultural historical theory: Implications for counseling and psychotherapy: Theory and practice. Talk given at the ISCAR congress, Seville, 2005.

Prilleltensky, I. (1997). *Critical psychology: An introduction.* London: Sage.

Quine, W. V. O. (1961). *From a logical point of view.* New York: Harper & Row.

Reifel, S. (1999). *Play contexts revisited.* Westport, CT: Greenwood.

Renesch, J., and Chawla, S. (2006). *Learning organizations: Developing cultures for tomorrow's workplace*. Portland, OR: Productivity Press.

Repkin, V. V. (2003). Developmental teaching and learning activity. *Journal of Russian and East European Psychology*, *41*(5), 10–33.

Resnick, M. D., Harris, L., and Blum, R. (1993). The impact of caring and connectedness on adolescent health and well-being. *Journal of Paediatrics and Child Health*, *29*, 83–89.

Rieber, R. W., and Robinson, D. K. (Eds.). (2004). *The essential Vygotsky*. New York: Kluwer Academic/Plenum.

Rieber, R. W., and Wollock, J. (1997). Prologue: Vygotsky's "crisis," and its meaning today. In R. W. Rieber and J. Wollock (Eds.), *The collected works of L. S. Vygotsky*, Volume 3 (pp. vii–xii). New York: Plenum.

Robbins, D., and Stetsenko, A. (Eds.). (2002). *Voices within Vygotsky's non-classical psychology: Past, present, future*. New York: Nova Science.

Robinson, K. (no date). From http://www.led.com/index.php/talks/ben_robinson_says_schools_kill_creativity.html, accessed 14 January 2008.

Rodgers, A., and Rodgers, E. M. (2004). *Scaffolding literacy instruction. Strategies for K-4 classrooms*. Portsmouth, NH: Heinemann.

Rogoff, B. (1990). *Apprenticeship in thinking: Cognitive development in social context*. New York: Oxford University Press.

Rogoff, B., and Lave, J. (1984). (Eds.), *Everyday cognition: Development in social context* (pp. 95–117). Boston, MA: Harvard University Press.

Rosen, H., and Kuehlwein, K. T. (Eds.) (1996). *Constructing realities: Meaning-making perspectives for psychotherapists*. San Francisco, CA: Jossey-Bass.

Rothstein, S. W. (1994). *Schooling the poor: A social inquiry into the American educational experience*. Westport, CT: Greenwood.

Sabo, K. (1998). The effectivenss of performatory developmental learning for teaching high school ESL. Report prepared for the Virgina Wellington Cabot Foundation.

Sabo, K. (2003). A Vygotskian perspective on youth participatory evaluation. *Youth participatory evaluation: A field in the making*. Special issue of *New Directions for Evaluation*, *98*, 13–24.

Sabo Flores, K. (2007). *Youth participatory evaluation: Strategies for engaging young people* (Research methods for the social sciences). San Francisco, CA: Jossey-Bass.

Salmon, P. (1980). *Coming to know*. London: Routledge.

Sampson, E. E. (1993). *Celebrating the other*. Hemel Hempstead, UK: Harvester Wheatsheaf.

Sawyer, R. K. (1997). *Pretend play as improvisation: Conversation in the preschool classroom*. Mahwah, NJ: Lawrence Erlbaum Associates.

Sawyer, R. K. (2000). Improvisational cultures: Collaborative emergence and creativity in improvisation. *Mind, Culture, and Activity*, *7*(3), 180–185. DOI:10.1207/S15327884MCA0703_05.

Sawyer, R. K. (2001). *Creating conversations: Improvisation in everyday discourse*. Cresskill, NJ: Hampton Press.

Sawyer, R. K. (2003). *Group creativity: Music, theater, collaboration*. Mahwah, NJ: Lawrence Erlbaum Associates.

Sawyer, R. K. (2004). Creative teaching: Improvisation in the constructivist classroom. *Educational Researcher, 32*(2), 12–20.

Sawyer, R. K. (2007). Creative teaching: Collaborative discussion as disciplined improvisation. *Educational Researcher, 23*(2), 12–20.

Schrage, M. (1999). *Serious play: How the world's best companies simulate to innovate*. Cambridge, MA: Harvard Business School Press.

Seikkula, J. (1993). The aim of therapy is to generate dialogue: Bakhtin and Vygotsky in family session. *Human Systems, 3*, 33–48.

Seikkula, J. (2003). Dialogue is the change: Understanding psychotherapy as a semiotic process of Bakhtin, Voloshinov, and Vygotsky. *Human Systems: The Journal of Systemic Consultation & Management, 14*(2), 83–94.

Seligman, M. (2002). *Authentic happiness: Using the new positive psychology to realize your potential for lasting fulfillment*. New York: Simon & Schuster.

Senge, P. M. (1990). *The Fifth Discipline: The art and practice of the learning organization*. New York: Currency Doubleday.

Senge, P. M., Kleiner, A., Roberts, C., Ross, R., and Smith, B. (1994). *The Fifth Discipline fieldbook*. New York: Currency.

Senge, P., Scharmer, C. O., Jaworski, J., and Flowers, B.S. (2005). *Presence: An exploration of profound change in people, organizations and society*. New York: Currency.

Shotter, J. (1989). Vygotsky's psychology: Joint activity in the zone of proximal development. *New Ideas in Psychology, 7*, 185–204.

Shotter, J. (1993a). *Conversational realities: Studies in social constructionism*. London: Sage.

Shotter, J. (1993b). *Cultural politics of everyday life: Social constructionism, rhetoric and knowing of the third kind*. Toronto: University of Toronto Press.

Shotter, J. (2000). Seeing historically: Goethe and Vygotsky's "enabling theory-method." *Culture and Psychology, 6*(2), 233–252.

Shotter, J. (2006). Vygotsky and consciousness as *conscientia*, as witnessable knowing along with other. *Theory & Psychology, 16*(1), 13–36.

Soyland, A. J, (1994). *Psychology as metaphor*. London: Sage.

Spolin, V. (1963). *Improvisation for the theater*. Chicago, IL: Northwestern University Press.

Spolin, V. (1975). *Theater games file*. Chicago, IL: Northwestern University Press.

Spolin, V. (1986). *Theater games for the classroom: A teacher's handbook*. Chicago, IL: Northwestern University Press.

Stern, D. N. (2000). *The interpersonal world of the infant: A view from psychoanalysis and development psychology* (2nd ed.). New York: Basic Books.

Stetsenko, A. (2004). Section introduction. Scientific legacy: Tools and sign in the development of the child. In R. W. Rieber and D. K. Robinson (Eds.), *The essential Vygotsky* (pp. 501–512). New York: Kluwer Academic/Plenum.

Strickland, G., and Holzman, L. (1989). Developing poor and minority children as leaders with the Barbara Taylor School Educational Model. *Journal of Negro Education, 58,* 383–398.

Strong, T., and Paré, D. A. (2004). (Eds.), *Furthering talk: Advances in discursive therapies.* New York: Kluwer Academic.

Sutton-Smith, B. (2001). *The ambiguity of play.* Cambridge, MA: Harvard University Press.

Terr, L. (1999). *Beyond life and work: Why adults need to play.* New York: Scribner.

Tharp, R. G. (1999). Therapist as teacher: A developmental model of psychotherapy. *Human Development, 42,* 18–25.

Tharp, R. G., and Gallimore, R. (1988). *Rousing minds to life: Teaching, learning and schooling in social context.* Cambridge: Cambridge University Press.

Toulmin, S. (1978). The Mozart of psychology. *The New York Review of Books, 25*(14), September.

Trevarthen, C. (1998). The concept and foundations of infant intersubjectivity. In S. Bråten (Ed.), *Intersubjective communication and emotion in early ontogeny* (pp. 15–46). Cambridge: Cambridge University Press.

Valsiner, J. (1995). Human development and the process of psychotherapy: Some general methodological comments. In J. Siegfried (Ed.), *Therapeutic and everyday discourse as behavior change* (pp. 81–93). Westport, CT: Greenwood.

Vera, D., and Crossan, M. (2004). Theatrical improvisation: Lessons for organizations. *Organizational Studies, 25,* 727–749. From http://oss.sagepub.com/ogi/content/abstract/25/5/727, accessed 1 December 2007.

Vygotsky, L. S. (1978). *Mind in society.* Cambridge, MA: Harvard University Press.

Vygotsky, L. S. (1987). *The collected works of L. S. Vygotsky, Volume 1.* New York: Plenum.

Vygotsky, L. S. (1993). *The collected works of L. S. Vygotsky, Volume 2: The fundamentals of defectology.* New York: Plenum.

Vygotsky, L. S. (1994a). The problem of the environment. In R. van der Veer and J. Valsiner (Eds.), *The Vygotsky reader* (pp. 338–354). Oxford, UK: Blackwell.

Vygotsky, L. S. (1994b). Imagination and creativity of the adolescent. In

R. van der Veer and J. Valsiner (Eds.), *The Vygotsky reader* (pp. 266–288). Oxford, UK: Blackwell.

Vygotsky, L. S. (1997a). The historical meaning of the crisis in psychology: A methodological investigation. In *The collected works of L. S. Vygotsky, Volume 3* (pp. 233–343). New York: Plenum.

Vygotsky, L. S. (1997b). *The collected works of L. S. Vygotsky, Volume 4.* New York: Plenum.

Vygotsky, L. S. (2004a). The collective as a factor in the development of the abnormal child. In R. W. Rieber and D. K. Robinson (Eds.), *The essential Vygotsky* (pp. 201–219). New York: Kluwer Academic/Plenum Publishers.

Vygotsky, L. S. (2004b). Dynamics and structure of the adolescent's personality. In R. W. Rieber and D. K. Robinson (Eds.), *The essential Vygotsky* (pp. 471–490). New York: Kluwer Academic/Plenum.

Weick, K. E. (2000). *Making sense of the organization.* London: Blackwell.

Wertsch, J. (1981). (Ed.), T*he concept of activity in Soviet psychology.* Armonk, NY: M. E. Sharpe.

Wertsch, J. V. (1985). *Vygotsky and the social construction of mind.* Cambridge, MA: Harvard University Press.

Wertsch, J. V. (1991). *Voices of the mind: A sociolcultural approach to mediated action.* Cambridge, MA: Harvard University Press.

White, M. (2007). *Maps of narrative practice.* New York: W. W. Norton.

White, M., and Epston, D. (1990). *Narrative means to therapeutic ends.* New York: W. W. Norton.

Wittgenstein L. (1953). *Philosophical investigations.* Oxford, UK: Blackwell.

Wittgenstein, L. (1965). *The blue and brown books.* New York: Harper Torchbooks.

Wittgenstein, L. (1984). *Culture and value.* Chicago: University of Chicago Press.

Wood, L., and Attfield, J. (1996.) *Play, learning, and the early childhood curriculum.* London: Paul Chapman.

Wood, D., Bruner, J., and Ross, G. (1976). The role of tutoring in problem-solving. *Journal of Child Psychology and Psychiatry, 17,* 89–100.

Yinger, R. (1980). A study of teacher planning. *The Elementary School Journal, 80,* 107–127.

Yinger, R. (1987). *By the seat of your pants: An inquiry into improvisation and teaching.* Paper presented at the annual meeting of the American Educational Research Association, Washington, DC.

Index